GARDENS OF THE LOIRE VALLEY

through the seasons

GARDEN • ART • PRESS

GARDENS OF THE
LOIRE VALLEY
through the seasons

INTRODUCTION BY *Hubert de Givenchy*

TEXT BY *Marie-Françoise Valéry*

PHOTOGRAPHY BY *Liz Eddison, Derek Harris, Gary Rogers,*

Derek St Romaine, Nicola Stocken Tomkins

Région

Centre

Dans le Centre, c'est vous le centre

UNESCO **VAL DE LOIRE**
PATRIMOINE MONDIAL

PARCS ET JARDINS
RÉGION CENTRE

Acknowledgements

The author and photographers would like to thank all the owners of the gardens visited for their assistance in making this book possible, together with the many gardeners, landscape designers and staff whose dedication made visiting and photographing the gardens such a pleasure.

They would like to express special thanks to Guillaume Henrion, President de l'APJRC, and Michele Quentin, also of the APJRC, for their help and advice whilst researching this book.

Our thanks also go to the Conseil Regional du Centre and UNESCO World Heritage for their support.

Marie-Françoise Valéry
Liz Eddison
Derek Harris
Gary Rogers
Derek St Romaine
Nicola Stocken Tomkins

THE ART OF LIVING AND CREATING

The Loire Valley between Sully-sur-Loire (Loiret) and Chalonnes-sur-Loire (Maine-et-Loire) has been inscribed on the list of UNESCO World Heritage Sites since 2000 as a living cultural landscape.

Divided into the Centre and Pays de la Loire regions, the Loire Valley bears witness to a harmonious development of interactions between human beings and their environment over two millennia. The landscape of the valley illustrates to an exceptional degree the ideals of the Renaissance and the Age of the Enlightenment on western European thought and design. It is equally remarkable for its architectural heritage.

The cultural landscape of the Loire Valley has been fashioned by man around the culture of four elements:

- The culture of water, with the Loire and its tributaries
- The culture of stone, with its built, architectural and monumental heritage (such as the Loire châteaux and abbeys) and its urban (the towns and villages built on the Loire) and domestic heritage (cave dwellings)
- The culture of gardens, both through ornamental gardens and the cultivation of fruit and vegetables
- The culture of wine and winemaking in the Val de Loire

The gardens of the Loire Valley form a remarkable facet of the living cultural landscape identified by UNESCO. An invitation to promenade, they are the elegant expression of a long tradition of aesthetic creation married with the pleasures of the kitchen garden. The 'art of the garden' has been elevated to a creative art in the Val de Loire, producing these dreamlike, idealised spaces halfway between man and nature.

The most famous sites, such as Villandry or Chaumont, take you on a voyage of discovery through fabulous gardens where tradition is married to modern ideas. Some, the jardins belvédères, set high above the Loire, offer spectacular panoramas over the royal river. Others, smaller and more intimate, blend simplicity and harmony.

For more information on the Loire Valley World Heritage Site visit: www.valdeloire.org

VAL DE LOIRE
PATRIMOINE MONDIAL

HERITAGE AND CREATION

The Loire is an exalted, subjugated river, whose universally recognised splendour has led to the transformation of the landscape and enriched the imagination of man. It is impossible to remain indifferent to the river's natural beauty, a challenge made even more difficult when this is complemented by the very finest of man's architectural achievements, when the frenzy of the Renaissance has taken hold of its châteaux, parks and gardens, when an entire territory has moulded its identity around the interaction between its people and environment.

Because it is permeated by the culture of the Loire Valley, the Région du Centre wished to put in place policies that would encourage the best possible results from the close interaction of creativity with the region's historical heritage.

Our objective is to preserve and enhance our cultural legacy but also to make it part of the art of today and tomorrow. To accomplish these aims, the Région has introduced a number of measures, in particular, aid for the restoration and creation of parks and gardens. This scheme enables the Région to provide support to owners – both public and private – to implement their projects, whether related to the development of the landscape or to cultural and artistic projects that revolve around the art of the garden.

This multifaceted policy allows the Région du Centre to encourage and sustain the work of all those involved in the creation and upkeep of gardens, the success of which is magnificently illustrated in this book.

François Bonneau
President of the Conseil Régional du Centre

Région

Centre

Dans le Centre, c'est vous le centre

GARDENS OF THE LOIRE VALLEY
through the seasons

TEXT BY MARIE-FRANÇOISE VALÉRY

PHOTOS BY LIZ EDDISON, DEREK HARRIS, GARY ROGERS, DEREK ST ROMAINE,

NICOLA STOCKEN TOMKINS

When the name of the Loire Valley is heard, many images spring to mind.

The Loire often flows with a certain languor, and it has conveyed gentleness and harmony to the landscapes that line its banks. Is this what persuaded the kings of France and their courts to establish themselves here? Their fascination with this river led to a unique architectural legacy, the fruit of the genius of artists from across Europe who gathered here to pool their artistic talents.

The cultural significance of this valley is one with its geography – they both seem infinite – and its inhabitants imbue it with a high quality of life and wealth of 'art de vivre'. Over the centuries the Loire Valley has become the Garden of France, an image that began to develop with the abbeys built here in the Middle Ages. This was furthered with a fresh impetus during the Renaissance, and has lasted till the present day. As the centuries have passed, some gardens have disappeared, others have fallen into a state of inactivity and await a new breath of life, but many continue and prosper, even today, to offer an image of perfection. And during recent years a series of new and innovative creations has appeared.

The 'Art du Jardin' remains a certainty in a society that is often led astray by mock facades. Nature is not deceitful! It evolves with the seasons, offering a permanently changing spectacle. In their own particular manner the gardeners in the Loire Valley each know how to get the best from their surroundings and to offer a magical extravaganza to the visitors who come here from all around the world.

I have always been very aware of the unique atmosphere in this region, which was itself one of the reasons I came to live here all those years ago. And, being so fond of the Loire Valley, how could I too not love its gardens in all their different aspects?

Reading or simply leafing through this book will allow you to share the beauty, serenity and happiness with which these places are endowed.

Hubert de Givenchy

CONTENTS

Drulon
Pages 112-119

Le Plessis Sasnières
Pages 146-153

La Source
Pages 180-187

La Fosse
Pages 120-125

Les Prés
des Culands
Pages 154-159

Talcy
Pages 188-193

Le Grand
Courtoiseau
Pages 126-133

Le Prieuré d'Orsan
Pages 160-165

Tours
Pages 194-199

Les Grandes
Bruyères
Pages 134-139

Le Prieuré de
St Cosme
Pages 166-171

Valmer
Pages 200-205

La Martinière
Pages 140-145

Le Rivau
Pages 172-179

Villandry
Pages 206-215

1. JARDINS DU CHÂTEAU d'AINAY-LE-VIEIL
18200 Ainay-le-Vieil
Cher
T: 02 48 63 50 03
E: chateau.ainaylevieil@free.fr
W: http://chateau.ainaylevieil.free.fr

2. PARC FLORAL d'APREMONT
18150 Apremont-sur-Allier
Cher
T: 02 48 77 55 00
E: info@apremont-sur-allier.com
W: www.apremont-sur-allier.com

3. ARBORETUM NATIONAL DES BARRES
45290 Nogent-sur-Vernisson
Loiret
T: 02 38 97 62 21
E: infos@arboretumdesbarres.com
W: www.arboretumdesbarres.com

4. PARC ET JARDIN DU CHÂTEAU DE BEAUREGARD
41120 Cellettes
Loir-et-Cher
T: 02 54 70 36 74
E: info@beauregard-loire.com
W: www.beauregard-loire.com

5. JARDINS DE LA VILLE DE BLOIS
Hotel de Ville
41000 Blois
Loir-et-Cher
T: 02 54 44 50 50

6. JARDIN DE BOIS RICHEUX
28130 Pierres-Maintenon
Eure-et-Loir
T: 06 11 88 20 20
E: contact@boisricheux.com
W: www.boisricheux.com

7. PARC ET JARDINS DU CHÂTEAU DE BOUGES
36110 Bouges-le-Château
Indre
T: 02 54 35 88 26
E: dominique.maldent@monuments-nationaux.fr

8. PARC ET POTAGER DU CHÂTEAU DE LA BOURDAISIÈRE
37270 Montlouis-sur-Loire
Indre-et-Loire
T: 02 47 45 16 31
E: contact@chateaulabourdaisiere.com
W: www.chateaulabourdaisiere.com

9. PARC ET POTAGER DU CHÂTEAU DE LA BUSSIÈRE
45230 La Bussière
Loiret
T: 02 38 35 93 35
E: chateaulabussiere@wanadoo.fr
W: www.chateau-labussiere.com

10. JARDINS DU CHÂTEAU DE CHAMEROLLES
45170 Chilleurs-aux-Bois
Loiret
T: 02 38 39 84 66
E: chateau.chamerolles@cg45.fr
W: www.loiret.com

11. LA PAGODE DE CHANTELOUP
Route de Bléré, 37400 Amboise
Indre-et-Loire
T: 02 47 57 20 97
E: info@pagode-chanteloup.com
W: www.pagode-chanteloup.com

12. JARDINS DU CHÂTEAU DE LA CHATONNIÈRE
Route de Langeais, 37190 Azay-le-Rideau
Indre-et-Loire
T: 02 47 45 40 29
E: deandia@aol.com
W: www.lachatonniere.com

13. DOMAINE RÉGIONAL DE CHAUMONT-SUR-LOIRE
41150 Chaumont-sur-Loire
Loir-et-Cher
T: 02 54 20 99 22
E: contact@domaine-chaumont.fr
W: www.domaine-chaumont.fr

14. PARC DU CHÂTEAU DE CHENONCEAU
37150 Chenonceaux
Indre-et-Loire
T: 02 47 23 90 07
E: info@chenonceau.com
W: www.chenonceau.com

15. PARC ET JARDIN DE CHEVERNY
41700 Cheverny
Loir-et-Cher
T: 02 54 79 96 29
E: domainedecheverny@chateau-cheverny.com
W: www.chateau-cheverny.fr

16. JARDINS DE DRULON
18170 Loye-sur-Arnon
Cher
T: 02 48 56 65 96
E: drulon@wanadoo.fr
W: www.drulon.com

17. PARC BOTANIQUE DE LA FOSSE
Fontaine-les-Côteaux
41800 Montoire-sur-le-Loir
Loir-et-Cher
T: 02 54 85 38 63

18. LES JARDINS DU GRAND COURTOISEAU
45220 Triguères
Loiret
T: 06 80 24 10 83
E: grand-courtoiseau@orange.fr
W: www.grand-courtoiseau.com

19. ARBORETUM DES GRANDES BRUYÈRES
45450 Ingrannes
Loiret
T: 02 38 57 12 61
E: fondation-mansart@wanadoo.fr
W: www.fondation-mansart.fr

20. ARBORETUM DE LA MARTINIÈRE
Rue du Lavoir, 37250 Veigné
Indre-et-Loire
T: 06 81 53 35 52
E: asso.arboretum@yahoo.fr
W: http://arboretum.micheldavo.com

21. JARDIN DU PLESSIS SASNIÈRES
Le Château
41310 Sasnières
Loir-et-Cher
T: 02 54 82 92 34
E: jardin.de.sasnieres@wanadoo.fr
W: www.jardin-plessis-sasnieres.fr

22. ARBORETUM DES PRÉS DES CULANDS
La Nivelle
45130 Meung-sur-Loire
Loiret
T: 02 38 63 10 49
E: parispierre2@wanadoo.fr
W: htpp://perso.orange.fr/houx/

23. JARDINS DU PRIEURÉ D'ORSAN
18170 Maisonnais
Cher
T: 02 48 56 27 50
E: prieuredorsan@wanadoo.fr
W: www.prieuredorsan.com

24. JARDINS DU PRIEURÉ DE ST COSME
37520 La Riche
Indre-et-Loire
T: 02 47 37 32 70
E: demeureronsard@cg37.fr
W: www.prieure-ronsard.fr

25. JARDINS DU CHÂTEAU DU RIVAU

37120 Lémeré

Indre-et-Loire

T: 02 47 95 77 47

E: info@chateaudurivau.com

W: www.chateaudurivau.com

26. PARC FLORAL DE LA SOURCE

45000 Orléans

Orléans-Loiret

T: 02 38 49 30 00

W: www.parc-floral-la-source.com

**27. VERGER DE COLLECTION
DU CHÂTEAU DE TALCY**

41370 Talcy

Loir-et-Cher

T: 02 54 81 03 01

W: http://talcy.monuments-nationaux.fr

**28. PARCS ET JARDINS DE LA
VILLE DE TOURS**

Hôtel de Ville

37000 Tours

Indre-et-Loire

T: 02 47 21 62 68

E: parcs-jardins@ville-tours.fr

29. JARDINS DU CHÂTEAU DE VALMER

Chançay, 37210 Vouvray

Indre-et-Loire

T: 02 47 52 93 12

E: jardins@chateaudevalmer.com

W: www.chateaudevalmer.com

**30. JARDINS DU CHÂTEAU
DE VILLANDRY**

37510 Villandry

Indre-et-Loire

T: 02 47 50 02 09

E: info@chateauvillandry.com

W: www.chateauvillandry.com

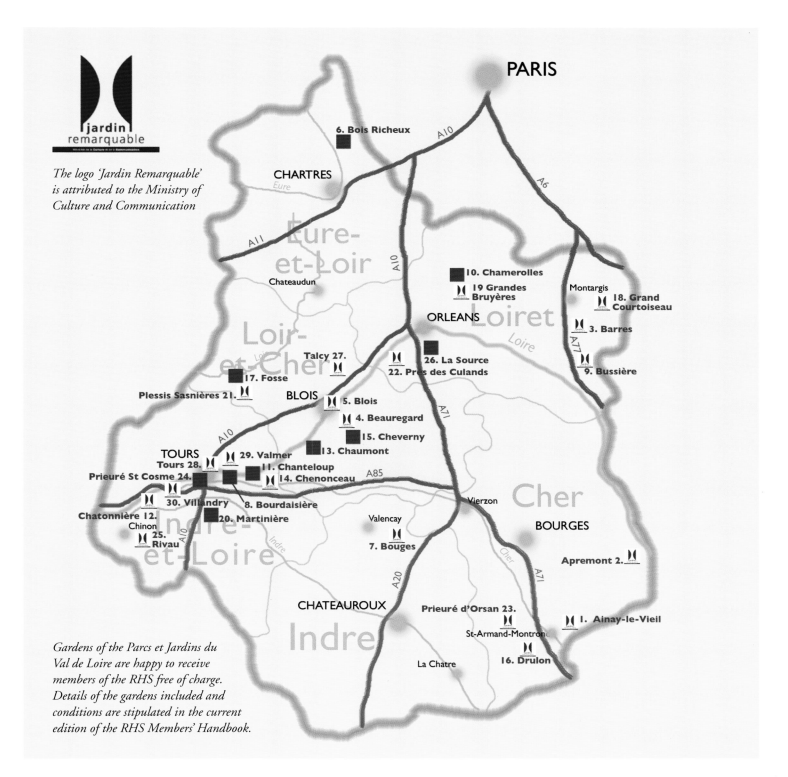

The logo 'Jardin Remarquable' is attributed to the Ministry of Culture and Communication

Gardens of the Parcs et Jardins du Val de Loire are happy to receive members of the RHS free of charge. Details of the gardens included and conditions are stipulated in the current edition of the RHS Members' Handbook.

AINAY-LE-VIEIL
Jardins du château d'Ainay-le-Vieil

PHOTOGRAPHY BY GARY ROGERS, DEREK HARRIS, DEREK ST ROMAINE AND LIZ EDDISON

Marie-Sol de La Tour d'Auvergne took on a wide-ranging project when she decided to restore the gardens at Ainay, and did so through her attachment to the place, or, as she puts it, 'for love of Ainay.'

Ainay is the château of her childhood: a medieval fortress – the 'Petit Carcassonne du Berry' – with its nine towers linked by ramparts, its Renaissance influence, its postern and its moats. As well as this, the chateau boasts landscaped grounds dating from the nineteenth century, remarkable trees, water channels, pools and fountains.

Marie-Sol was obliged to replant the park, "the maintenance of which had been handed over to the animals", but then a major climatic event occurred: the famous storm of 1984 that assailed northern France and southern England. The trees in the park fell one after another, but what could be done in the wake of such a disaster? Should it be replanted in exactly the same manner?

She pondered, researched the possibilities and documented her findings, uncertain of the right path to follow. One particular encounter, however, was to determine the course of events: her meeting with Pierre Joyaux, a nurseryman and landscape gardener. "He had just the right passion and talent," she explains. "We began by creating a rose garden in front of the chateau, we moved the cows and sheep out, made our plans and planted."

The rose garden is her masterpiece. Its charming design is based on seventeenth-century pavilions. Its yew topiaries are trimmed into forms that are both dignified and unpretentious, and its circumference is lined with small compartments, formed by walls of hornbeam. The water channels murmur and glint, and tall trees offer their protection. The gentle shades of the colours are brought out even more through their contrast with the imposing buildings. The layout is simple and classic, revealing both a knowledge and understanding of roses.

The rectangular rose garden is both geometric and symmetric, formed around two paths that intersect at the centre. The longer of the two paths is lined along its entirety by climbing roses entwined around three-legged supports. At each end the path extends to form a circle: one lined with the same columns and climbing roses, the other with trimmed hornbeam. The overall rectangle of the rose garden contains smaller rectangles of closely packed and carefully labelled rosebushes. The grassy paths stretch from one side of the garden to the other, allowing the visitor to wander right across to better observe the flowers. The shorter path, also lined with climbing roses, leads to other gardens.

The roses were chosen for their colours, with the emphasis on gentler tones. Placed under the protection of linden and plane trees that filter the light, they were selected to tell a story: the story of the rose.

It starts with botanical rosebushes (that is to say, wild roses that nature has given us), in this case *Rosa sericea pteracantha*, easily recognised by its long, red, translucent thorns. The story continues with Gallic roses. Though their origin is mysterious, they are probably the oldest of the ancient roses; *Rosa gallica* is a member of this family. Next come the Damask roses, of which the most famous is 'Madame Hardy', white with a green eye. White rosebushes follow, *Rosa* x *alba*, with the famous 'Cuisse de Nymphe' (Nymph's Thigh). Then the *Centifolia* enter the stage with 'Chapeau de Napoléon' (Napoleon's Hat), which resembles *Rosa centifolia* with its marvellous scent, and is one of Marie-Sol's favourites. The roses of China and Bourdon, and the Tea rosebushes are irresistible. They are followed by the modern remontant hybrids, the polyanthas and the floribundas. And finally, the famous English Roses.

Ainay is also home to the botanical curiosity, *Rosa viridiflora*, a green rose that is perfect for a bouquet. Deserving of special notice is the Rose Colbert, named at Ainay in 1989; this species was created by Delbard in honour of Louis XIV's finance minister, who was an ancestor of the owner's family. It is described as: "A two-coloured rose, creamy white with a hint of porcelain pink that darkens as it blooms." It has won several prizes at international competitions.

On leaving the rose garden, we climb a few steps and cross over a small water channel to reach the other gardens. There is a lot of water at Ainay – moats, channels, a stream and a fishpond – once crucial features that either helped to defend or sustain the chateau, but which soon became harmonious elements of its décor. The channels were created in the eighteenth century around an immense kitchen garden; this no longer exists, but has been turned into the Jardin de l'Isle. "The kitchen garden was ringed with water. It was designed in the nineteenth century to have four large vegetable areas lined with flowers. Exposed fruit trees were planted along the water channels. All that has disappeared. We have created hornbeam enclosures along one of the cross avenues that leads to the Chartreuses. In the middle of this avenue we have set out a 'pond' planted with blue perovskias and white 'Fée des Neiges' (Iceberg) rosebushes," explains Marie-Sol.

Next we enter the 'Chartreuses de Montreuil', a remarkable structure formed by a row of small, high-walled, individual gardens similar to those in Canon, Normandy, which was so sheltered from the wind that fruits used to be grown there.

The Jardin Bouquetier is, for the most part, planted with hardy perennials that flower year after year. It shows an acknowledgement of William Robinson and Gertrude Jekyll, who last century introduced a wave of revival to the art of gardening through their judicious use of herbaceous plants. In this part of the garden we find lady's mantle (*Alchemilla*), sea kale (*Crambe maritima*) and stone crop (*Sedum*), as well as rosebushes and hydrangeas. From here the view over the row of small, enclosed gardens is very lovely.

The Verger Sculpté is innovative and daring, and demonstrates the art of training and pruning fruit trees. Inspired by the magnificent work of Jean de La Quintinye, the brilliant creator of the Potager du Roi at Versailles, the trees take on a marvellous variety of shapes: here we find goblets, fans, palmettes verriers, pyramids and candelabras.

The Jardin de la Méditation revolves around a fresco inspired by Giotto, in which St Francis is seen talking to the birds. A house in hornbeam, borders of box *(Buxus)* and germander *(Teucrium fruticans)*, staggered rows of blackberry bushes around a pool, and the music of a fountain all contribute to the creation of an atmosphere suited to meditation.

The Cloître des Simples is ringed by a gallery of linden trees with four square beds of plants in the centre. These are used for medicinal, aromatic, tinctorial and melliferous purposes that diffuse their delightful scents.

The Parterres de Broderie tribute to Le Nôtre and the gardens of the seventeenth century. The tone is set by carefully pruned box, volutes and trellis work. The walls are lined with espaliers of roses and clematis. The branches of a Judas tree *(Cercis siliquastrum)* are trained into the shape of a fan.

Each of these special gardens captures the attention and intrigues the viewer, making a visit to Ainay a unique experience.

RIGHT *The intricate patterns, painted trellis work and iceberg roses of the Parterre de Broderie.*

ABOVE *The moated château of Ainay-le-Vieil in early spring.*

RIGHT *Yews* (Taxus baccata) *planted into Versaille boxes and trained into obelisks line a path bordered by hornbeam.*

OPPOSITE TOP LEFT *The rose garden looking towards an outbuilding and tiered topiary yews.*

OPPOSITE BOTTOM LEFT *Four rectangular knots in the meditation garden.*

OPPOSITE RIGHT *A fresco of St Francis feeding birds in the meditation garden seen through the framework of an umbrella shaped lime tree and living willow hedge.*

OPPOSITE TOP LEFT *Seating area underneath the canopy of umbrella shaped lime trees with a rectangular pool behind clad with ivy.*

OPPOSITE BOTTOM *An archway leads from the fruit garden into the meditation garden.*

LEFT *Pear trees are trained in an arch across a wide path in the fruit garden.*

ABOVE *Looking through an archway into the fruit garden.*

APREMONT
Parc floral d'Apremont

PHOTOGRAPHY BY DEREK HARRIS

Apremont is a universe apart. A protected microcosm. A well-loved village that has remained intact.

A country road that runs along the river Allier is dotted with Berrichon houses, each with their own small gardens, and remarkably well designed topiaries in hornbeam and yew. They are striking, but they respect the proportions of the place, being simple yet extremely elegant. Who could have visualised them there, other than someone with finesse, imagination and a knowledgeable eye?

The scene has been set. The shapes are formed by the ribbon of the river, the large trees, a church tower and the motif of tiled roofs – often with four sloping sides – half Berrichon, half Burgundian. On a hill stands an impressive chateau overlooking a large garden, which answers back just as strongly from below. The colours are provided by the brown of the tiles, the ochre of the wall-plaster, the green of the English-style lawns, the grey of the slate tiles on the château, the lively hues of the flowers. The textures range from the rusticity of the materials in the hamlet to the sheen of the seigniorial roof; there are also shimmering ponds, a delicate mass of fragile petals and an infinite variety of leaves. Further on, the houses and topiaries soon pass beyond the park railings, leaving you unsure whether you are in a village or a garden; the two blend into one another.

Here, in the face of all opposition, including that of his family, Gilles de Brissac decided to

put his talents as a landscape architect to the test with the creation of a 'parc floral', which would enable him to share the fruit of his labour with as many people as possible. Gilles derived his refined taste in gardens from his grandmother, Antoinette de Saint-Sauveur, who became Madame Schneider by marriage. He spent his youth in the enchanted gardens of his grandparents, where he was initiated into the world of English gardens. It was from his grandparents that he inherited Apremont, through the intermediary of their daughter, the Duchesse de Brissac. Pursuing the work of his grandfather – who, on the advice of the architect Galea had selected which houses in the hamlet should be preserved, demolished or rebuilt – Gilles de Brissac threw all his energies into safeguarding the authenticity of the village that lies at the foot of the chateau.

Following Gilles' death in 2002, his sister, the writer Elvire de Brissac, who shares her brother's extensive knowledge of the gardening world, took the reins. Under her skilful direction, with respect for its spirit and setting, the garden has been maintained in perfect condition. And yet it has developed – for a garden evolves due to the force of nature, and gardeners are repeatedly obliged to adapt to its laws by cutting back branches, for example, or controlling the growth of a copse to retain the beauty of a carefully fashioned view.

"The garden will be fifty years old in 2010," Elvire tells us. "Gilles used to say that it took fifty years for a garden to settle in. Now it has

settled! It has found its place in the locale and the climate." With her gardener Tony Poupin, she constantly strives for greater perfection and tries to create a subtle harmony between the seasons, blossoms, scents, heights and colours. "Gilles achieved all this from just a meadow. I so much admire the imagination and foresight that it took," Elvire continues. "He was very inspired by England and it was his goal to create an English garden in our local Berry landscape."

"He conceived it like a visionary. With Charles de Noailles, Russell Page and Jaqueline de Chimay, in the 1970s he was one of the first to feel that the era of the garden was arriving. He was a sort of pioneer. Far ahead of others, he understood that everyone needs beauty and that a garden has a remarkable power of inspiration. His plan was very ambitious. Only his grandmother looked kindly upon it. He carried it through to a successful conclusion due to his love of gardens and botany."

We enter the garden through the old village square. "There used to be a road that ran past this building, Gilles bought it up and included it in the garden," Elvire de Brissac explains. In front, a green carpet worthy of the best Scottish golfing greens provides the link between the different elements, an achievement made possible only by the knowledge that the climate at Apremont is close to that of Switzerland and Germany, and a long way from the warmth of the Gulf Stream. An elegant silk tree *(Albizia julibrissin)* catches the eye: its finely serrated,

mimosa-like leaves and pink feathery blooms are usually found in the south-west of France, but clearly it is also able to resist the winters in Apremont! The tree precedes the spring border which is a mass of colourful narcissi, hyacinths and innumerable tulips, blended with simple plants like columbines, poppies and peonies.

The promenade passes beneath a long pergola, originally conceived by Gilles de Brissac as "a waltz in triple-time. With the wisteria on the first bowers, robinias on the second, laburnum on the third, and repetitions of this order." However, the laburnum wouldn't take in the local soil, so Gilles had to abandon this idea and replace them with roses. When the flowers are in bloom at the same time, the combination of Chinese and Japanese wisteria (*Wisteria sinensis* and *W. floribunda*) and bristly locust acacia (*Robinia hispida*) produces a magnificent effect. It is so spectacular in May that anyone visiting at another time of year should return then simply to experience the sight of the flowers and the 'tunnel of scents' they produce.

By a small house in the Apremont style, Gilles de Brissac created a cottage garden with a profusion of perennials that blossom in summer: irises, lupins, phlox, hardy geraniums and asters are mixed with dahlias, punctuated by gigantic, architectural plants such as hollyhocks, *Macleya cordata* and castor oil plants (*Ricinus*). The walk then continues towards the Belvédère, which marks the highest point in the garden, and offers a superb view over the valley, château and ponds. Inside, Nevers faïence panels in the style of sketches by Alexandre Serebriakoff depict a journey around the world, passing through Africa, the Indies, Oceania and China, finally to arrive in…Apremont!

Returning downhill, we are led towards the waterfall where enormous rocks act as a springboard for the water that gushes down the slope. Its very scale provides a direct measure of the ambitiousness of the achievement. After this we pass through plantations of rare trees that prosper in this region to such an extent that they form a magnificent arboretum. These trees arrived at Apremont in pots when the park was first created, and have now achieved their full majesty: liriodendrons, cypresses, liquidambars, *Quercus palustris*, and several varieties of maple, such as *Acer brillantissimum*, blaze magnificently with colour in the autumn. The theme of water is echoed in a series of ponds inspired by those at Sheffield Park. Approaching them, we pass three cows grazing peaceably on the path that leads to a second folly: the floating Turkish Pavilion. The

interior is illustrated with a series of paintings by Jacques Roubinet of the different ages of life, enhanced by the interplay of mirrored reflections.

The promenade continues over the fully restored Chinese Bridge and reaches the White Garden, modelled on the one at Sissinghurst in Kent. Here Gilles de Brissac planted a profusion of bulbs and hardy perennials: hyacinths and tulips with grey-leaved santolinas and artemisias, and perennials such as bellflowers, irises, phlox and Japanese anemones, whose blooms continue right into autumn. He included several boxwood domes that, like paper-weights, were intended to have the effect of calming and ordering the profusion of flowers and foliage. The scene is set against a backdrop of a hornbeam hedge trimmed into pyramids that ring a green stage and allow the gaze to escape towards the roofs of the village.

Whether consciously or not, Gilles de Brissac's creation has affinities with Château de Groussay in its buildings, and with the whimsicality of Biddulph Grange on account of its Chinese Bridge, but also with the Queen's Hamlet at Versaille, Portmeirion in Wales, and Blaise Hamlet near Bristol. However, due to its scale it remains unique in France, as Apremont is a living village in which neatly labelled perennials flourish in every patch of ground, and every house, including those inside the park, is inhabited.

LEFT *The colourful promenade in May with flowering wisteria and the small Apremont style cottage.*

RIGHT *The view from the top of the waterfall over the lake and the Chinese Bridge to the commanding château.*

ABOVE *Garden well with climbing clematis, petunias and geraniums in the White Garden.*

RIGHT *Flower detail of heleniums.*

OPPOSITE *The spring border with its colourful display of daylilies, dahlias, roses, hibiscus, achillea and salvia.*

OPPOSITE TOP *The Belvédère: the highest point of the garden and offering a superb view of the river.*

OPPOSITE BOTTOM *The decorated interior of the Belvédère with ceramic panels by Alexandre Serebriakoff depicting a journey around the world.*

LEFT *The floating Turkish Pavilion on the tranquil lake with interior decoration by Jacques Roubinet.*

ABOVE *The long pergola in May, a tunnel of flowering Chinese and Japanese wisteria (Wisteria* sinensis *and* W. floribunda).

LEFT *A summer view across the lake to the Chinese Bridge and parkland beyond.*

ABOVE *The White Garden with boxwood cones and the hornbeam hedge trimmed into pyramids.*

RIGHT *Cows grazing peacefully in the plantation of rare trees.*

FAR RIGHT *The winding path up to the Belvédère.*

LES BARRES
Arboretum National des Barres

PHOTOGRAPHY BY DEREK HARRIS

 The Arboretum National des Barres is internationally famous, though its location is less well known, lying between Montargis and Gien in the area of the Gâtinais. The arboretum is associated with the famous École Forestière, and therefore with the illustrious Vilmorin family.

Vilmorin is a name often heard in the world of plants, for example *Cryptomeria japonica* 'Vilmoriniana' is a compact dwarf conifer ideal for rockeries, *Davidia involucrata vilmoriniana* was brought back from China by Fargès in 1897, and *Potentilla* 'Vilmoriniana' is one of the best potentillas there is: it stands straight, its flowers are a creamy white and it has silvery leaves.

In particular the Vilmorins have been famous for several centuries for dealing in seeds, and their shop in Paris, on the banks of the Seine, has contributed to their renown.

Their home is Verrières-le-Buisson in Essonne is surrounded by a marvellous collection of rare trees. Russell Page, who was a friend of André de Vilmorin, described Verrières in *Education of a Gardener*: "The Vilmorins have been a family of horticulturists and seed merchants for two centuries and for generations have lived in the Château de Verrières south of Paris. There, over the centuries, around a delightful Louis XIV building, whose garden contains a see-saw that once belonged to Louise de la Vallière, the Vilmorin family has created a series of gardens,

laboratories and trial fields where the seeds are tested... It has always been a family business."

Their descendant, Jean-Baptiste de Vilmorin, has continued that tradition and is director of the Société Nationale de Protection de la Nature at the Museum d'Histoire Naturelle, and in 1991 published a book called *Le Jardin des Hommes*, which tells the history of plants. This book is not only a compendium of his knowledge and education, but also his outlook enriched by several decades of experience and wisdom handed down from father to son.

The Vilmorin name is closely attached to a sophisticated botanical culture, and to a refined, elegant and courteous mind, as Madame de Bassompierre described in her portrait of her uncle Philippe-André (1776–1862): "He was gentle and cheerful, knew English perfectly, played the violin and so enjoyed telling the fables by La Fontaine – whom he resembled in his continual absent-mindedness – each evening until the end of his life he used to recite them with infinite grace and charm in the sitting-room at Les Barres…"

It was Philippe-André who bought Les Barres in 1821. His aim was to bring together plants from all over the world, in particular small shrubs and trees, both broad-leaved and persistent, to observe and compare them. He made this arboretum into a unique collection, now known around the world.

It was the soil here that attracted him to Les Barres. The different types of soil on the property enabled him to study the behaviour of

a single species or variety planted in different types of earth, for instance acidic and chalky.

He also carried out research into fodder plants and had a beet named after him: 'La Jaune Ovoïde des Barres'. His descendants, as well as the École Forestière (created in 1873), continue his work.

The Valmorin collection was based on plants from the four corners of the world, collected and brought back by missionaries and botanists, such as Jean Delavay, Charles Sprague Sargent and Paul Guillaume Fargès, whose names have all been remembered in the plant world.

When walking through the Arboretum, one should bear in mind the intentions of its creator: his desire to observe, appreciate and classify every specimen.

Anyone with an interest in trees should visit the Arboretum National des Barres: this conservatory teaches us to love and appreciate trees, to distinguish between deciduous and evergreens – something that seems elementary – but also to recognise those that fall between the two: for example, the ginko (*Gingko biloba*), which loses its leaves despite being related to conifers, and the larch (the *Larix* family), which is a conifer that sheds its foliage.

You will also learn which trees are native and which have been introduced from far afield and had to acclimatise to a new setting.

You will learn to understand the difference between opposite, alternate, grouped, naked and hairy buds. The buds of deciduous

magnolias (either *Magnolia* x *loebneri* or *M. stellata*) can easily be identified in winter as they are covered with a silvery downy sheath. As for the chestnut tree, its metamorphosis each year is quite astonishing, as its buds contain flowers and leaves that develop in the wink of an eye.

You will come to recognise the different types of leaves: simple, compound, ovate, dentate, cordate, lobate, fan-shaped and palmate, purple and variegated. And the green, yellow or blue needles found on conifers.

You will learn to identify trees by their catkins or blossom, whether these are discreet or spectacular, like that of the Japanese flowering cherry, the magnolia, the hawthorn, handkerchief tree (*Davidia involucrata*) and the tulip tree (*Liriodendron tulipifera*). Or perhaps by their fruit, whether red like the holly and sorb, more sophisticated like the hybrids of the same species, black like certain types of rose trees, or fawn like the medlar.

You will marvel at their seeds, whether round or winged, and at their colours in autumn, notably the elegant, flaming maples, and the spindle-trees that take on beautiful raspberry hues.

The Arboretum National des Barres is a living catalogue of species and a place of education. To understand it properly it is best to visit all three of its collections.

The Geographic Collection groups trees by their origins: in Europe, the Americas (planted in the nineteenth century), and

Asia (introduced to Les Barres at the start of the twentieth century). Take a moment to appreciate the maples, which have very attractive barks, for example *Acer pensylvanicum* has a green bark with reddish-brown stripes, and foliage that turns a bright yellow in autumn; *Acer davidii* has green bark veined with white and leaves that turn orange in autumn; whereas *Acer griseum* loses its bark to produce thin brown strips.

The Ornamental Collection holds rare species appreciated for their unusual and aesthetic qualities, like a *Thuja* with twenty-four trunks, and botanical curiosities created by man's intervention. The Bizarretum brings together the twisted hazel tree (*Corylus avellana* 'Contorta'), with its curiously distorted branches and leaves, the weeping cedar of Lebanon (*Cedrus atlantica* 'Pendula') and the linden tree with laciniated, shredded leaves (*Tilia platyphyllos* 'Laciniata').

The Systematic Collection (across the road) classes the plants by family: there are trees, of course, but also the shrubs classified and grouped in the Fruticetum at the end of the nineteenth century by Maurice de Vilmorin, thanks to seeds brought back from abroad by missionaries. All the specimens are organised in beds as though it were a kitchen garden. Here you can see the first handkerchief tree (*Davidia involucrata*) to have been introduced to Europe (by Père Fargès). In May its flowers are completely hidden by very beautiful creamy-white oval bracts.

The walk comes to an end when you return towards the two new buildings at the entrance. These buildings – one representing a beechnut and the other an acorn – were designed by contemporary architects to be in keeping with the very essence of Les Barres.

ABOVE *A misty morning in autumn, on the way to the Ornamental Collection, a carpet of pink and white cyclamen.*

FAR LEFT TOP *The bark of a lichen and moss covered tree.*

FAR LEFT BOTTOM *An autumn coloured glade of young maples in the Geographic Collection.*

MIDDLE *A wonderful full autumn coloured maple in the Geographic Collection.*

ABOVE *A colourful pathway in the Systematic Collection with young maples in autumn colours.*

LEFT *Small detail of fallen maple leaves.*

FAR LEFT *A winding path on a misty autumn morning through a glade of beech trees.*

ABOVE *Cyclamen covering the floor of a dense woodland glade near the Ornamental Collection.*

LEFT *A sunlit glade through an avenue of beeches.*

RIGHT *The clean air of Les Barres allows lichen to grow everywhere; this jewel could be easly missed.*

BEAUREGARD
Parc et jardin du château de Beauregard

PHOTOGRAPHY BY LIZ EDDISON AND DEREK ST ROMAINE

"Beauregard the well-named: though hidden from indiscreet gazes and protected in its peaceful haven behind the forest of Russy, Beauregard offers its occupants views over the calm Beuvron valley and the small pretty church of Cellettes. Close to Blois, Chaumont and Chambord, it does not attempt to rival its royal cousins in either size or magnificence, but can offer the interested visitor the elegance of its architecture and the beauty of its setting."

This is how the Comte Alain du Pavillon described his beloved Beauregard. Today, his wife carries on the work of restoration, with improvements to the gardens very much at the heart of operations. In 2000, her strong love of roses was attested by the creation of the rose 'Château du Beauregard' by Sauvageot, characterised by a fruity scent and tightly grouped cream flowers tinged with cherry-red. Beauregard the well-named, and the well-loved!

After passing through the thick forest of Russy, the long avenue bordered by enormous balls of box and maple comes as a welcome relief. The recently planted maples, magnificent in autumn, took the place of overly elderly fruit trees. On the other side of the Renaissance residence is a long carpet of green, where a very fine fleur-de-lys of fine gravel stands out against the lawn. Nearby, the 'Vertugadin', or 'Farthingale', is planted with oaks, cotinus, St-John's-wort and dogwood.

Close to the outbuildings stands the Chambre des Parrotias. Persian ironwood (*Parrotia persica*) is a tree that rarely grows straight above its trunk. Its leaves resemble those of the beech and take on magnificent golden, flame-coloured hues in autumn.

For a better understanding of the gardens it is worth visiting the château. Beauregard has a noble history and its paths and steps have been crowded with famous people. At one time it was a hunting lodge belonging to François I; Richelieu and Louis XIV also visited. On no account miss an engraving that shows the château and its gardens in all their magnificence as they were in the sixteenth century. This is taken from a remarkable work called *Les plus excellents bâtiments de France* by the famous Jacques I Androuet du Cerceau (1510–1585). An architect, draughtsman, engraver and poet, Androuet du Cerceau published engravings of the most beautiful examples of French Renaissance architecture and their gardens – including the châteaux of Anet, Chantilly, Amboise and Beauregard – in this four-volume work, most of which are seen from a bird's eye view. The work was commissioned by Catherine de Medici, who is closely associated with the history of the nearby Château de Chenonceau.

At that time the château was centred around an internal courtyard and was surrounded by gardens. Laid out geometrically, they were elegant, harmonious and well-proportioned. Close to the château were square flowerbeds, which most likely contained medicinal plants.

It is also mentions that the building stood among vineyards and fruit trees; clearly all its plantations were designed primarily for utility rather than pleasure.

The tour of the château is completed by a visit to the Galerie des Illustres. This exceptional gallery, dating from the sixteenth century, is lined with portraits of the kings of France, their ministers, constables and marshals, as well as figures who played a role in foreign affairs. The gardens also pay tribute to famous individuals.

The old kitchen garden was transformed into the Jardin des Portraits in the 1990s by the landscape gardener Gilles Clément. Access to the garden is by a monumental flight of steps embellished with a mosaic in the form of a compass rose that stands close to a fountain. The garden is divided into twelve chambers enclosed by hedges of trimmed hornbeam; each section is represented by its own colour and is dedicated to a famous man or woman. The Jardin des Portraits is a garden of artifice. It is laid out geometrically in straight lines but its chambers are joined to one another by a winding path. The entrances linking the chambers do not face one another but are staggered. Even though the chambers are all the same size, the winding path makes some appear larger, others smaller. At the centre of each chamber stands a tree, the colour of its foliage declaring the chosen colour of that section. Thus, the luminous golden foliage of a 'Sunburst' *Gleditsia triacanthos* denotes that

yellow is the colour of its chamber, in which calliopsis, 'Gold Plate' *Achillea filipendulina*, Missouri primrose (*Oenothera missouriensis*), and Yellow loosestrife (*Lysimachia punctata*) are planted at random, and a 'Golden Wings' rosebush cheers the end of spring with its yellow blooms. This chamber is dedicated to Louis XIII, the father of the Sun King. The white chamber, where a 'White Rock' (*Philadelphus* 'Pekphil') stands out, pays tribute to the white feather worn by François I so that he "would be recognised in the midst of battle". The black chamber, crowned by a 'Royal Purple' cotinus, is in the colours of Diane de Poitiers, who wore only black and white all her life. The pink chamber commemorates the 'Rose of Prosvins' as "Anne de Bretagne, the wife of Charles VIII, then Louis XII, used the rose essence produced at the Abbey of Prosvins". The dominant plant in this section is the 'Yang-Tse' *Lagerstroemia*. The blue chamber, dressed with 'Henri Desfossé' *Ceanothus*, represents the Order of Saint-Esprit. All the chambers are planted with a profusion of perennials.

At the end of the Jardin des Portraits stands a rockery of dwarf conifers, featuring the densely leaved *Pinus mugo* and 'Nana' *Pinus strobus*. You will want to see the rose 'Château de Beauregard', which stands in the company of ancient roses like 'Charles de Mills' and 'Jacques Cartier' and a selection of their English colleagues. The walls of the ancient kitchen garden are also lined with espaliered rosebushes.

From here the garden leads up towards the Verger des Écorces (lit. Orchard of Bark), which is planted with prunus, spindle-trees (*Euonymus*), which sometimes have unusual barks, and maples (including *Acer griseum*) which exfoliate. In the distance one can see an old ice-house undergoing restoration. The promenade continues past the cedar grove, where the recently planted *Cedrus libani*, *C. atlantica* and *C. deodara* are instantly recognisable, and then past the man-made pond featuring an assortment of grasses and water lilies; the very lovely pink flowers of the 'James Bridon' *nymphea* stand out.

Heading back towards the château, a path lined with beautiful holly trees (*Ilex castaneifolia*), with their wide, soft and glossy leaves like those of a chestnut-tree passes through the Bois des Chênes (Oak Wood). The oaks are clearly labelled, allowing easy recognition of *Quercus dentata*, a small tree with large deeply lobed leaves, and *Quercus hispanica*, a vigorous tree with marcescent foliage.

You then have to walk back past the château to see the Jardin de la Chapelle, which dates from earlier than the fifteenth century, on the ruins of which climb a California flannelbush (*Fremontodendron californicum*), a climbing plant with large yellow flowers that appreciates a warm, sheltered situation. This is a cool, shady garden where the large trees protect heathers, camellias (including the famous *Camellia sasanqua*, which blooms in autumn), hydrangeas, ferns, pieris, Heavenly bamboo (*Nandina domestica*) – whose fruits are very lovely in autumn – and rhododendrons that cheer the undergrowth in spring. This is a pocket of humiferous earth, an exception at Beauregard, where the soil is chalky.

ABOVE *The avenue to the château lined with clipped buxus.*

FAR LEFT TOP *The château set amongst its grounds.*

LEFT *Detail from a statue in the parkland.*

BELOW *The ruins of the chapel.*

RIGHT *Roses growing around a door in the courtyard.*

TOP FAR RIGHT *Cedar of Lebanon in the parkland.*

BOTTOM FAR RIGHT *Decorative terrace inlaid with points of the compass and fountain.*

ABOVE *Verbascum,* Alchemilla mollis *and conifers in the Green Chamber.*

RIGHT *Planting in the Black Chamber including* Cotinus Coggygria *'Royal Purple',* Foeniculum vulgare *'Bronze'.*

ABOVE *The conifer garden which sits beyond the 'Jardins Des Portraits'.*

LEFT Foeniculum vulgare *'Bronze' and* Lysimachia ciliata *'Firecracker' planted in the Black Chamber.*

BLOIS
Jardins de la ville de Blois

PHOTOGRAPHY BY LIZ EDDISON AND DEREK ST ROMAINE

 Blois is certainly a very lovely town. From the opposite bank of the Loire, the sight is of the river slipping past like a ribbon, a line of carefully trimmed plane trees, the district of St Jean with its slate mansard roofs, and the terraces that climb the hill towards St Louis's Cathedral and the Episcopal Palace. It is on the terrace of the bishop's palace that the Roseraie is laid out.

To appreciate the gardens as a whole, their design and the sequence of green chambers, it is best to look down from near the statue of Joan of Arc. From this point the view over the Loire and its bridges is magnificent. Everything is in harmony: the slate roofs are as silvery as the river, and as grey as the foliage in the Jardin des Cinq Sens (Garden of the Five Senses), which acts as an antechamber to the Roseraie. And the brick-built chimneys are as pink as the countless roses that bloom on the terrace below.

THE JARDIN DES CINQ SENS This is also on a terrace and overlooks the roofs of the St Jean district and the other terraces planted in times past with fruit trees. It is a gentle garden of blue and white flowers and grey foliage. Lavender, nepetas, bell-flowers, hardy geraniums, *Iris germanica*, globe thistles and ceanothes provide the blue; iberis, more bell-flowers, *Hibiscus* 'Diana' and *Exochorda racemosa*, the white; and stachys (*Stachys lanata*), rue (*Ruta graveolens*), lavender, and oleaster (*Elaeagnus* x *ebbingei*), the grey.

It is a sight to delight the eyes, but what of the remaining four senses? The sense of touch is tested by the contrasting impressions from the stinging leaves of the thistles and the soft, woolly feel of the stachys. The sense of smell is delighted by the scents of the lavender, thyme and rosemary. And while the gentle music of a waterfall charms the ears, the cordons of apples and palmettes of pears standing against the sun-warmed walls tempt the tastebuds. The fruit varieties include 'Gros Loquard' and 'Cramoisie de Gascogne' among the apples, and 'Louise Bonne d'Avranche' and 'Duchesse d'Angoulème' amongst the pears.

THE ROSERAIE Philippe Coupechoux assists Nathalie Bernard in caring for the City of Blois gardens, both in selecting plant varieties and in taking creative decisions. He remarks, justifiably, that the city is very lovely in winter, an important fact as "Blois is only in leaf for six months a year".

"Winter has the merit of emphasising the architecture of the buildings and of the plants. The structural branches of the rosebushes are visible. The beech trees, with their strongly horizontal lines, are very apparent with their lovely marcescent leafage. The small fruits of the *Malus* 'Everest', whose vertical lines are very evident, are beautiful when rimed with hoar-frost. And it is easier to make out the round heads of the Steppe Cherry, *Prunus fruticosa* 'Globosa', which line the terrace and coat it with a white cloud in spring."

In winter the composition of the Roseraie – designed by Arnaud Maurières and Eric Ossart – stands out very clearly. The first chamber is coloured white and cream with roses such as 'Penelope' and 'Fée des Neiges'. It is characterised by a circular motif, which is echoed in the round pool at the other end of the terrace.

The second chamber – laid out in lines parallel to the Loire – is filled with yellow, orange, bi-coloured and pinkish roses, such as 'The Fairy' and 'Kathleen', while the third chamber intermingles pink and red roses, including 'Tapis Rouge', 'Lavender Dream' and 'Red Parfum'.

The fourth retraces the history of the rose from its origins to the modern hybrids. The bushes, planted in beds that ring the circular pool, are classed by families. Here you will find botanical roses, the roses of Portland, Gallic roses, coarse roses, and Chinese roses.

The immense walls of the Roseraie are espaliered with climbing roses with spectacular blooms, like the 'Maria Lisa', mixed with clematis. And the lovely *Clematis tangutica* prolongs its gorgeous yellow feathery blooms from autumn into winter.

The City of Blois has implemented a plan for biological protection of its plants as part of a wide-ranging suppression of chemical treatments. As part of this scheme, predator insects, such as the syrphus fly, green lacewing and ladybirds, have been introduced to counter the threats posed to the gardens' roses by pests.

THE CHÂTEAU GARDENS The gardens lie close to the château in the heart of the city, on the site of a deep, redeveloped ditch where the landscape gardener Gilles Clément created three new gardens during the 1990s.

The Jardin des Fleurs Royales dominates the town. Spread across a terrace, it is dressed by a gallery of hornbeam shaped into archways and diagonal ribs like the royal gardens of the past, and three lines of a chessboard, the centre square of which is a water pool. The other squares are planted with hemerocallis ('daylilies'), as the lily is an emblem of royalty.

The Jardin du Roi has a geometric design featuring wave-shaped hedges with alternating peaks and troughs, giving the sensation of movement. The hedges are interspersed with tall plants such as grasses, hemp, willow sunflower (*Helianthus salicifolius*), clary sage (*Salvia sclarea*), and roses – *Rosa chinensis* 'Mutabilis', with its flowers that fade from light to dark pink, and *Rosa rubrifolia*, which has bluey-green leaves and small pink flowers.

The Jardin des Simples is designed as a chessboard surrounded by paving; the plants in the squares are either medicinal or aromatic: artemisia, tansy, digitalis, mallow, mint and sage. The whole garden is enclosed by hornbeam hedges into which 'windows' have been cut to give a series of views of the town.

RIGHT *Views of the Loire with* Prunus fruticosa *lining the terrace beside the rose garden.*

OPPOSITE TOP *A small herb garden beside the top terrace of the Episcopal Palace.*

OPPOSITE BOTTOM *The view of the Roseraie, the Episcopal Palace and the Loire from the statue of Joan of Arc.*

MIDDLE *The Jardin des Cinq Sens with* Stachys lanata *on one side of a grassy pathway.*

ABOVE *Steps lead down into the Jardin des Cinq Sens.*

LEFT *A pergola in the Roseraie.*

ABOVE *The top terrace of the Jardin des Fleurs Royales with its lines of square beds and archways of hornbeam.*

RIGHT *Cherry blossom.*

MIDDLE *Four crab apples* (Malus) *in blossom.*

OPPOSITE *Hedges of* Taxus baccata *(yew) make graphic wavy diagonal lines across the square with cherry and crab apple in blossom and the imposing château in the background. The garden was designed by Gilles Clément and built above an underground car park.*

BOIS RICHEUX
Jardin de Bois Richeux

PHOTOGRAPHY BY NICOLA STOCKEN TOMKINS

 Charles Péguy sang the praises of the Beauce. You have to learn to love it: neither still nor monotonous, it has its rhythms, moods and seasons, its periods for sowing and harvesting, its crops that sway in the wind. Stretching to the horizon, the ground seems to touch the sky, with even the spires of the cathedral of Notre-Dame in Chartres – visible from miles around in this "ocean of wheat" – seeming to act as a link between the two.

The garden of Bois Richeux is very much in keeping with this unity. It too lies between earth and sky. Alix and Hubert Mourot wanted it that way. In this place where history is traced back to the Middle Ages, they have created a garden of medieval inspiration: contemporary but timeless. They have given it a spiritual dimension. Like all medieval gardens, it is enclosed, but with doors and windows so that it can also be opened up to the outside world.

"We were looking for a family house not far from Paris. When we visited Bois Richeux, Hubert was immediately and powerfully struck by the close link between the material and the spiritual. Something that had to be brought out. I looked into the history of this feudal farm, Hubert designed the garden, and I helped by improving my knowledge of botany," Alix Mourot relates. Being respectively a painter and a stylist, Hubert and Alix both have a trained eye with regard to form, style, colour and volume, so they composed a simple but refined chequered garden designed down to the smallest detail.

The Medieval Farm of Bois Richeux is "one of the oldest farms in Beauce and an important site for the freedom of the peasants in the twelfth century," explains Alix Mourot. "It was at that time that the Lord of Bois Richeux donated part of his land to the Chapterhouse of Chartres Cathedral so that the first non-feudal farmers could establish themselves there. This event is recorded in a very ancient manuscript from 1178."

There is also a description of the farm in the ancient records of Notre-Dame de Chartres; Alix Mourot walks us through it: "You enter through the present gateway crowned by a postern. The manor-house stands at the centre of the courtyard, its walls built from string courses of brick and flint mortar set on a solid foundation formed of twelfth-century blocks of sandstone. The tithe barn stands opposite. The number of pigeonholes in the dovecote

indicates that the worked area of the farm at that time covered more than 1100 hectares. The cowsheds set behind the manor-house have disappeared. The fruit shed still stands above the ancient 'enclosure' (in other words the prison), attesting to the rights of the high, middle and low justices of the lords of Bois Richeux. A kitchen garden lay between the walls, with its vine arbour and beds framed by woven osiers where flowers, and edible, medicinal and aromatic plants are grown."

In the seventeenth century, the farm and its lands were bought by Madame de Maintenon and were then in 1679 incorporated into the Château de Maintenon. And thus it remained until the arrival of Alix and Hubert Mourot.

The garden of Bois Richeux is already very lovely in winter, standing out clearly against the background of the sky. All the plants are very evidently pruned and cared for. Their gentle, elegant half-tones are in perfect harmony with the woodwork and stones of the manor-house, with all the tonalities of green and grey represented. The lavender, rosemary and thyme run alongside the box or yew. The cobblestones and woven edging harmonise with the sandstone, brick and flint of the manor-house.

The garden is laid out with simplicity, following the chequered motif that was very much in vogue in the Middle Ages. It is formed by square beds, raised to encourage growth as the soil – lined on all four sides by cobblestones, box or osiers – is easily warmed.

Hubert Mourot explains that the layout of

the garden was created automatically by simply aligning its axes with the windows of the manor-house. Nonetheless, two difficulties had to be overcome: first, as the courtyard was not level, it was necessary to create terracing so that the squares would appear flat; secondly, the squares had to fit into the trapezium formed by the positions of the buildings. Through judicious trimming and use of perspective, the impression is given that the squares are laid out in a courtyard with four right angles.

The square beds containing medicinal plants lie next to the dovecote: absinthe, sage, oregano and poppy are appreciated here for their curative properties. They treat the body and, perhaps, the spirit too. "It is an open-air pharmacy," as Alix Mourot likes to say.

The squares of aromatic plants are close to the entrance of the manor-house. "The collections of lavender remind us that people in the Middle Ages were very clean and took several baths a week in warm water infused with lavender, thyme and rosemary, all of which are invigorating, soothing and at the same time anti-bacterial." There are also tinctorial plants like pastel (or woad, *Isatis tinctoria*) and scented plants such as clary sage, which is also very beautiful. These squares are lined with rounded hedges of box.

Laid out in two lines that intersect at a clover-leaf pool to form a cross, the squares containing edible plants are bordered with woven osier. The plants themselves – broad beans, cabbage, lettuce, fennel, Swiss chard and marrow – are altered each year to follow the principles of crop rotation, and to ensure they are colourful as well as tasty.

The chequerboard is closed on one side by a hornbeam cloister that stretches from the Chambre d'Amour to the Chambre de Méditation, and on the other by a chestnut arbour entangled by a climbing vine (or rather a chasselas grape), honeysuckle and a hop. The start of this medieval structure lies close to the ancient chapel of St Gilles.

The spiritual dimension of the garden is expressed in the symbolism of the plants: *Lilum candidum* – the Madonna lily, *Alchemilla mollis* – Lady's mantle, and carnations, columbines, irises, roses and daisies, which are all represented in illuminations of sacred gardens. The cross is present in the design of the kitchen garden and in the interplay of vertical and horizontal lines. The scents too represent a path to heaven; and the two spirals traced out in yew, between which you have to pass to reach the door to the manor-house, symbolise life, movement and infinity. The exuberance of the squares in summer is countered simply with spaces or intervals, designed to illustrate the difference between emptiness and solidity. These interludes in the design of the courtyard correspond to the silences in music that give value to harmonies and chords; silence of course being one of the fundamental themes of monastic life, to encourage elevation of the soul towards God.

Finally, at Bois Richeux the square is in continual relationship with the circle, like matter and spirit, the earth and the firmament. This truly is a garden for the body and spirit, a garden between earth and heaven!

LEFT *Capturing the spirit of medieval gardens, herbs and vegetables fill raised beds edged in woven willow.*

RIGHT *Researched by owners Hubert and Alix Mourot, this courtyard of 68 square beds recreates the austere but refined spirit of medieval gardens.*

ABOVE AND LEFT *Box-edged beds filled with medicinal, culinary and aromatic plants, are grouped around informal plantings of lavender, salvia, santolina and fennel.*

RIGHT *The ancient dovecote and the original buildings from this medival farm create a calm back-drop to the 68 square beds that fill the courtyard.*

FAR LEFT *The early spring face of the garden, its herbs and box hedges clipped in readiness for spring, seen from the cloister of hornbeam.*

TOP *At the foot of the dovecote, a box-edged bed overflows with white arabis.*

LEFT *Woven willow hurdles form a raised bed filled with red lettuce.*

RIGHT *Stripped of leaves in early spring, the tranquil, hornbeam cloister is divided into small cubicles by low box hedges.*

BOUGES

Parc et jardins du château de Bouges

PHOTOGRAPHY BY LIZ EDDISON, DEREK ST ROMAINE AND DEREK HARRIS

In order to fully appreciate Bouges, you have to imagine the flat countryside of Berry: it is rustic and austere, with hardly a tree growing. The hedges have been erased from the landscape. Even the places along the road have expressive names: 'Les Deserts' on one side and 'La Beauce' – after the monotonous and treeless plain in central France – on the other.

Not far from here – in a coomb reached by following a lovely bridal path – a pleasant setting can be found, its entrance marked by balls of mistletoe, suspended from high branches of ancient poplars. And there, lying in front of you, past generations have succeeded in creating the best possible example of French sophistication. Balance, elegance, refinement and harmony have, on a small scale, been given

material form by a talented architect in order to enrich the life of a small village community. The château's administrator, Madame Dominique Maldent, describes Bouges as a hidden treasure or "jewel in a box". It is Madame Maldent who, with her sophisticated flower arrangements, perpetuates the 'art de vivre' of the estate's last private owners, Monsieur and Madame Viguier, and so keeps the place alive.

First, there is the house. The contrast between the Berry landscape and this eighteenth-century work of art is striking. The building is reminiscent of the Petit Trianon, or the Château de Canon in Normandy. Constructed to replace a fortified manor-house, of which almost nothing is known, its design is attributed to Gabriel. Since then, a variety of owners have left their mark on the Château de Bouges and its gardens through a series of transformations, embellishments and restorations.

The house was built by the Marnaval family in 1756. Then, during the Restoration at the start of the nineteenth century, a landscaped park was created, featuring a pond, plantations of local trees, and sinuous contours. In 1857 the property was bought by the Dufours, who commissioned Henri and Achille Duchêne (father and son) to re-design the park and gardens. Monsieur and Madame Viguier bought the estate in 1917. Their hard work to restore the compositions laid out by the Duchênes made this the 'golden age' of Bouges,

until the sad death of Henri Viguier in 1967.

The gardens are designed along two axes. The first, running east-west, follows the Allée Cavalière, which is planted with plane and chestnut trees, and crosses the Cour d'Honneur (reception courtyard), which is lined with linden trees, and features low lines of box and a mosaic of brick and stone. It then passes next to the house and continues its course around a *buffet d'eau* fountain and pool – in which the house is reflected – before continuing along a carpet of grass lined with truncated pyramids of yew. Here the view opens out onto the trees in the park, the only interruption coming in the form of a monument, which has been positioned at the focal point of the perspective.

The north-south axis starts from the old vegetable garden, which Madame Viguier transformed into the Jardin Bouquetier (flower garden). It then passes through the glasshouses, cuts through the stableyard and the courtyard for the servants' quarters, crosses the house and the bed planted with box, and extends towards the pond. Continuing in this direction, the eye is drawn onwards to the English-style park; this has been planted with tulip trees from Virginia, larches, Corsican pines, bald cypresses and liquidambars, which take on magnificent hues in the autumn.

The parterre de broderie, or knot garden, at Bouges is unique. It matches the style of the château and is an integral, almost indespensible, part of the whole place. According to French gardening tradition,

the parterre de broderie must be situated so that it can be admired, like a carpet, from the windows high above. It must also lead the gaze beyond, towards the horizon. And this is just the way it is at Bouges.

When you walk in this part of the garden, the pond appears to be very near to the parterre de broderie. In fact the architect has contrived a very clever optical illusion, giving the impression that the parterre dominates the pond situated below, when in fact it is much further away. This juxtaposition of the highly elaborate parterre with the natural feature of the pond is one of rare beauty.

According to eighteenth-century tradition, parterres de broderie must be laid out geometrically and symmetrically. They should be planted with volutes and arabesques of box, suggesting foliage and florets, and should stand out against a coloured surface such as sand, coal, crushed tiles or lawn. At Bouges the trimmed box stands on top of fine gravel, and is surrounded by a perimeter made up of cone-shaped yew and rows of linden trees. The beauty of this small, intimate and sophisticated French garden is raised to new heights by frost or snow in winter.

Dominique Maldent manages the domain with competence and enthusiasm. Among her responsibilities are the flower arrangements, and she works closely with head-gardener Gilles Barnier on this task, as he is responsible for the Jardin Bouquetier, or flower garden. Since the time of Madame Viguier, whose idea it was to transform the vegetable garden into the Jardin Bouquetier, a specialist has paid regular visits to advise on which species to plant there.

Enclosed by walls, the Jardin Bouquetier is crossed by two paths, which meet in the middle at a round pool. Both paths are lined with a variety of roses: 'Queen Elizabeth', 'Iceberg', 'Tapis Rouge' and 'The Fairy'. The large glasshouse is home to tropical and Mediterranean plants such as banana and lemon trees; the small glasshouses are used for seedlings and re-potting. The flowers – marigolds, balsams, heliotropes, periwinkles, salvia, nigellas, and bellflowers – are grown here in beds, as they would be in a vegetable garden, and all are at their brightest and most colourful in summer.

At Bouges the bouquet season continues throughout the year. Even in November, a difficult month, Dominique Maldent succeeds in matching her flower and leaf arrangements to the wallpaper of the drawing room, and to the most beautiful fabrics and silks of a seat or wing chair. To complement a blue and pink flowered pattern, for example, she mixes pink hydrangeas and abelias, blue-grey eucalyptus and white snowberries with foliage of spiraea, to create a wonderful harmony of colours.

When the Viguiers still lived at Bouges, flowers would be sent from the gardens every week to decorate the family home in Paris. And each morning, Monsieur Viguier would have a carnation brought to him on his breakfast tray to use as a buttonhole. The essence of this refinement endures at Bouges today. Every detail there reminds us of the care and attention that has been invested in the park.

LEFT *Detail of colourful border with* Zinnia elegans.

RIGHT *The walled Jardin Bouquetier, or Flower Garden, in summer with trimmed box borders and roses, marigolds, dahlias, geraniums and salvia.*

OPPOSITE *The pattern made by the box parterre de broderie* (Buxus sempervirens) *viewed from above and flanked by conical shaped yews* (Taxus baccata).

ABOVE *The pool, fountain and yew topiary.*

RIGHT *Detail of a garden ornament.*

LEFT *The reception courtyard viewed from the terrace above.*

ABOVE *An avenue of lime trees on the terrace above the Cour d'Honneur.*

RIGHT *Lime trees on the terrace above the Cour d'Honneur.*

OPPOSITE FAR LEFT *The small greenhouse containing exotic plants, tropical and Mediterranean, including banana plants, lemon trees, philodendron, lantana and begonias.*

ABOVE *The central pool with containers of fuchsia and verbena.*

OPPOSITE LEFT, LEFT AND TOP *The walled Jardin Bouqetier with colourful flowering box-trimmed beds.*

LA BOURDAISIÈRE

Parc et potager du château de La Bourdaisière

PHOTOGRAPHY BY NICOLA STOCKEN TOMKINS, GARY ROGERS AND DEREK ST ROMAINE

 For some years now, La Bourdaisière has been enjoying life once more. Dynamism, optimism, bright colours, elegance and respect for a certain "art de vivre" are the keywords. Today, thanks to the brothers Louis-Albert and Philippe-Maurice de Broglie, who bought the property at the start of the 1990s, the place is as well known for its extraordinary collection of tomatoes as for its château and park.

The estate is a mix of styles and epochs, confirming the eventful history of the château and its park. Louis-Albert de Broglie notes

that this place was the setting for a procession, or ballet, of "beautiful roses", as it witnessed the presence of Marie Gaudin, the mistress of François I, and her grand-daughter, Gabrielle d'Estrées, a favourite of Henri IV, who was born at La Bourdaisière.

The château was originally a medieval fortress, having been built to defend the area around Tours. Today only one tower and the moats, now dry, to the north and east of the château are left. Having been transformed into a country residence, it welcomed through its doors, among others, the King of France, François I. In the seventeenth century, the château was enlarged and three fine outbuildings, which are still standing, were added.

Eventually the estate fell into the hands of the disgraced Duc de Choiseul, who had been exiled to his nearby château of Chanteloup. It was he who ordered the château at La Bourdaisière to be demolished. In the eighteenth century, the estate having changed hands again, the château was replaced with a solid, cubic construction, several paintings of which survive.

By the start of the nineteenth century La Bourdaisière was owned by Baron Angelier, who had the château renovated in the neo-Renaissance style that we see today. He filled in the moats, did away with all surviving medieval constructions, created the kitchen garden, and transformed the gardener's house into a lovely neo-Gothic chapel that today is fronted by a

charming little box garden planted with roses and topiary.

Passing by the chapel, you come to the château, the outbuildings and the park. The grounds are still characterised by the design it was given by Edouard André (1840–1911), the renowned landscape architect and botanist who was very active in this region. As was the fashion at the time, André planted clumps of trees of the same species. From the edge of the terrace in front of the château it is possible to admire these large trees, which bestow the estate with such nobility, in particular, the copses of cedars of Lebanon, which have a rare elegance.

A note of equal refinement is given by the Fleur de Lys just below the terrace. This was designed in the 1930s by Louis Descorges as part of his overhaul of the entire park at that time. The image is created by arabesques that interlace balls of box trimmed to a size suited to the Renaissance château that overlooks it. The curves and swoops of the design suggest movement and dynamism, and are outlined with santolinas and rosemary.

It is worth taking the path into the more wooded section of the park to find the Porte Italienne, which is attributed to the hand of Leonardo da Vinci. Then return towards the outbuildings to discover the kitchen garden where Louis-Albert and his brother Philippe-Maurice de Broglie have set themselves the goal of recreating the smells and flavours of their childhood. This colourful rectangle – the most

original feature at La Bourdaisière and a superb example of good taste and the "art des jardin" – is an homage to the tomato.

It was in Asia, India in particular, that Louis-Albert discovered tomatoes that he had never seen in France and which, to boot, were also tastier than he had ever experienced. This gave him the idea of seeking out different species and forming a collection. First, he purchased a large number of seeds and plants in Asian markets and asked botanic gardens and collectors around the world to swap seeds. Then he applied himself to the task of growing them, studying them and protecting those species and varieties that were either unknown or in danger of disappearing. The climate at La Bourdaisière was perfect for the task, and so the kitchen garden was returned to its primary task with the addition of this marvellous miscellany of tomatoes. "This was how this collection of rarities came into being, in collaboration with the Association Kokopelli, which protects bio-diversity and champions the presence of ancient varieties in our gardens; curiosities to be preserved, known and passed on," explains Louis-Albert de Broglie. It has even led to a book on the subject, written in partnership with Dominique Guéroult, called *La Tomate d'hier et d'aujourd'hui.*

The kitchen garden covers a hectare and its design merits appreciation. It lies on a slight incline that slopes down towards the outbuildings, in the past vines were cultivated here. It is enclosed by walls that protect and maintain the warmth of the plants. The garden is entered through an attractive old gate that opens directly onto an arbour draped with roses. Two large paths cross at right angles at the centre beneath a gazebo, thus cutting the garden into the traditional four large squares which are then each subdivided into four further squares. The layout of each of the smaller square varies: some are symmetrical, others asymmetrical or circular; some have transversal beds but in others they may be diagonal or zigzagging. All are designed with the aim of introducing diversity and, above all, of allowing the tomatoes to be observed from close up, helped by the small pathways that lead into the beds.

In the distance, a very lovely eighteenth-century glasshouse can be seen undergoing state-of-the-art restoration.

All the tomatoes are cultivated by the head gardener Nicolas Toutain without the use of chemicals. The collection, which was begun in 1995, now numbers more than 600 varieties and has been recognised as a "collection agréée" by the Conservatoire des Collections Végétales Spécialisées. The tomatoes are cultivated in the company of herbs: here you will find ten varieties of thyme and fifty of basil. These rarities – red, orange, yellow, and variegated white, green, pink and almost black – grow surrounded by flowers typical of kitchen gardens, like large purple amaranths, bright red dahlias, and coppery or golden sunflowers, all joyously trapping the sunshine of Touraine.

LEFT *A collection of different varieties of basil* (Ocimum basilicum) *in terracotta pots.*

RIGHT *The potager of this sixteenth-century castle is planted with herbs, vegetables, flowers and 550 varieties of heirloom tomatoes.*

TOP *On a grassy hillside lies a formal parterre of huge box domes edged in lavender.*

ABOVE *View through a gateway to the château.*

RIGHT *Carpet of cyclamen beneath the trees.*

FAR RIGHT *Ancient woodland surrounds the château and in autumn the chestnut trees turn golden brown.*

RIGHT *Prince Louis Albert de Broglie, châtelain of the estate at La Bourdaisière shares his passion for tomatoes.*

BELOW *A glass vegetable 'forcer' with melons.*

BOTTOM RIGHT *Yellow Stuffer tomatoes.*

MIDDLE *Some of the heirloom and unusual tomatoes cultivated at La Bourdaisière with names such as Zakopane, Burracker's Favourite, Grinta and Gold.*

FAR RIGHT *Acudens Purple tomatoes.*

LA BUSSIÈRE

Parc et potager du château de La Bussière

PHOTOGRAPHY BY LIZ EDDISON AND DEREK ST ROMAINE

The origin of the word Bussière seems to be related to the Latin buxeria, derived from *buxus*, meaning 'a place planted with box'. Consequently, the idea is conjured up of a château rich in history, built of ancient worked and patinated stone, standing in verdant surroundings. Visitors to La Bussière should explore both the house and the important *potager* (vegetable garden), which has recently been restored by Geneviève de Chasseval, with the help of her children and grandchildren.

Today, the château is striking for its beauty and nobility, having traversed the centuries rather as a ship might ride the waves. The lake provides a shimmering sheet of water on which the château seems to float, making it sparkle incessantly. The changing sky is reflected there, endowing the château with life and movement all year round. Initially built as a medieval fortress, it became a country residence at the end of the sixteenth century. Then in the seventeenth century a walled park, attributed to Le Nôtre (1613–1700), was added. All that remains of this early design are the long rectilinear paths – set out in the form of stars ending in ditches, or ha-has – the symmetry and simplicity of their design epitomising the spirit of French parks.

These principles were later reinterpreted by the landscape designer Edouard André (1840–1911). "My husband's grandmother invited André to restore the gardens," explains Madame de Chasseval. "He was a friend of the Vilmorin family that lived at Les Barres near Nogent-sur-Vernisson. The River Vernisson passes through the lake, leaves the park and heads towards Nogent before flowing into the Loing at Montargis. It's all connected. It was Edouard André who planted the mushroom-shaped topiaries in the courtyard. My husband inherited the domain in 1959." It has taken a lot of energy, determination and fervour to bring the place back to life.

"In the past our family used to be extensive. More than fifty people lived here and they were fully self-sufficient," Geneviève continues. "We are in Puisaye and the ground is clay. There used to be an oven here made of bricks and their colour would change with the cooking time. The three immense granaries in the barn were used to store the estate's harvests." This accounts for the barn built from pink bricks, interspersed with black ones to form diamond-shaped patterns.

There has always been a fruit shed on the property: "The apples can be stored there until the strawberries are picked in June!" recounts Madame de Chasseval. She visits the shed once a week to ensure that only the healthy fruit is conserved; this avoids any risk of mould passing from one fruit to another. Amongst the different varieties grown, 'Reine des Reinettes', 'Calville Rouge', 'Reinette du Mans', and 'Clochard' are the most outstanding. The pears are stored in the same way as the apples, but they are picked when they are green and then allowed to ripen on their trays; they go by the names of 'Cuisse de Dame', 'Triomphe de Vienne', 'Doyenné du Comice', 'Comtesse de Paris', and 'Sucrée de Gien', a local variety. All of these fruits are grown in either the potager (or kitchen garden) or in the dry defensive ditches.

It is the delightful vegetable garden – dating from the eighteenth century – that has brought fame to La Bussière. "We have not altered its layout at all," Geneviève explains. "It was a useful place that provided not only fruits and vegetables, but also the flowers for the flower arrangements for the château and the church."

The vegetable garden lies close to the main gateway, flanked by the two Louis XIV pavilions. The first sight of the garden is from above – five stone steps down lead to a closer look. From the initial position of elevation, you can appreciate the harmony of the garden's design: enclosed by walls which provide enough shelter for delicate fruits such as figs and peaches to ripen, its rectangular shape narrows slightly (like the central path) towards the end to create the illusion of length. It is set out in squares and is equipped with a glasshouse (also dating from the nineteenth century), a well, a rose-covered pergola and a tunnel of mixed cucurbits: pumpkins, Turk's-cap, winter squash and bitter apples.

The central path is lined with rows of fruit trees and 'Little White Pet' and 'Fée des Neiges' roses. On either side the garden is organised in squares. Here you will find 'Maman Turbat' roses, a polyantha created in 1911 by Eugène Turbat, a rose-developer and Mayor of Orléans. One square is given over to vegetables, where carrots compete with lettuces and cabbages, creating an attractive mix of form and colour; another contains just fruit – redcurrants, raspberries and blueberries. A third square is dedicated to medicinal plants: absinthe to soothe the intestines, nettles for rheumatism, chicory for digestion, digitalis to treat heart failure, and violets and castor oil plants as purgatives.

Madame de Chasseval's aim is to create a gentle harmony between textures and colours, placing emphasis on pink and white to match the bricks of the buildings. In the late autumn the remontant roses, castor oil plants, Japanese anemones, asters and dahlias bestow a great deal of cheer on the vegetable garden.

The walk continues into the 'English Garden', which is dotted with cabins: the woodcutter's cabin has been built around an ash tree, the fisherman's hut is made of logs and stands at the water's edge, another is made from living reeds and so 'develops' as it continues to grow. And on an ancient rise, stands a structure made from the park's acacia trees.

We rejoin the linden-lined path that runs alongside the pond, and pass before a pocket handkerchief-sized lawn that garnishes a small overhang projecting from the drainage ditches. And then, finally, the monumental gateway.

RIGHT *Pumpkins, cactus dahlias and gaura in the potager enjoying the last rays of evening sun.*

ABOVE *White and red cactus dahlias enclosed in hedges of lavender in the potager.*

RIGHT *Espalier apples trained on wires.*

CENTRE *Russet apples being trained on a bamboo frame in the potager with winter squash ripening on beds of straw and massed planting of dahlias and gaura.*

OPPOSITE TOP RIGHT *Ruby chard and Australian chard.*

OPPOSITE BOTTOM RIGHT *Tunnel of gourds.*

ABOVE *View of the château from across the lake.*

RIGHT *Flowers of* Ricinus communis, *the castor oil plant.*

MIDDLE TOP *Trompe l'oeil on a wall near the entrance to the château.*

MIDDLE BOTTOM *A rustic bridge over a stream leads into the woodland.*

OPPOSITE *A meadow of cosmos in an area designed for children.*

CHAMEROLLES
Jardins du château de Chamerolles

PHOTOGRAPHY BY DEREK HARRIS, LIZ EDDISON AND DEREK ST ROMAINE

The charm of Chamerolles is apparent at first glance. Arriving from Courcy-aux-Loges, you see the château nestled in the surrounding woods, completely at one with its setting, as though it has always been there. If, however, you arrive from the other side, from Neuville-aux-Bois, then you are struck by the contrast of the surrounding wilderness with the beauty of the estate's imposing, elegant, well proportioned and carefully regulated trees and plants. They unquestionably form a masterpiece of green architecture, conceived by a trained eye, and maintained to perfection by a head gardener who understands and loves plants and who knows how to treat them.

Though the moats, drawbridge, and towers of this fortified château speak of the

uncertain times of the Middle Ages, the influence of the Renaissance can clearly be seen in the treatment of its façades. Its walls are embellished with pink and black diamond-shaped patterns in the brickwork typical of the Loire Valley, the windows are edged with white tufa, and the whole exterior is adorned with decorative motifs showing an Italian influence. The building was originally constructed in the twelfth century, and then renovated by Lancelot du Lac, a rich member of the court of Louis XII, between 1500 and 1530.

In the sixteenth century, French gardens developed from being simply useful, as they had been during the Middle Ages, to giving pleasure too: they were endowed with imaginative flowerbeds, full of colour, blooms and their scents. They were designed to give satisfaction to both the senses and the spirit, and plants hitherto unknown were imported from distant lands. Chamerolles became an expression of all these novelties, uniting utility, harmony and display.

More recently the château and gardens have been restored by the chief architect of Historic Monuments, Jacques Moulin. His basic design is based on a simple drawing dating from 1777, which shows a rectangle surrounded by a ditch and divided into six squares. In order to make sure his planting was in keeping, he consulted *Les plus excellents bâtiments de France* by Androuet du Cerceau, some engravings taken from the *Songe de Poliphile* by Francesco Colonna, original planting contracts, literary

texts and engravings of the gardens of royal palaces.

The gardens are reached via the moat. Once across, you are attracted by a walkway beneath the large bowers lining the two long sides of the garden. From here you are afforded a view of all six squares, all the while remaining in the protective shade of the trelliswork – as protecting one's skin from the sun was of concern to the fashionable ladies and gentlemen of the period.

The arbours are typical of this era of transition between the Middle Ages and the Renaissance. Formed by three splendid structures made from the exotic hardwood nyangon, they cover a wide path with a succession of arches supporting all sorts of climbing plants: wisteria, honeysuckle, voluble polygonums, vines and a hop intertwined with rose-bushes like 'Sir Cedric Morris', with its simple, pure white flowers, and 'Etoile de Hollande' with its velvety scarlet blooms.

The six squares are enclosed by chestnut and iroko trellises and are laid out in three sections to symbolise three aspects of existence: the first two squares represent aesthetics; the middle two, intellectualism; and the last two, utility.

The first, on the left, is a 'préau' cut by squares of grass, and with four grass-covered brick benches. This area was used as an outdoor salon where one could sit on the benches and pass the time of day. All around the edge of this little garden runs a flowerbed planted with columbines, sage, rosemary

and Madonna lilies. Botanical roses, like *Rosa spinosissima,* and ancient roses, like *Rosa centifolia,* complete the scene and add to the sweet and powerful perfume.

To the right of this garden is a square with an obelisk at its centre point. Recreated from the drawings by Androuet du Cerceau, it is ringed by a hedge of box, outside of which lies a much larger square divided into triangular beds embroidered with plants.

The second section of squares features a yew maze whose twists and turns eventually lead to a beech tree at its centre. Mazes were a popular feature of gardens at the time and may have been attributed with a spiritual connotation.

On the right lies a bed of rare plants. It was here that, in the sixteenth century, the lord of the château planted his collection of botanical curiosities being introduced at the time from such places as the Americas and the Mediterranean basin. Star-shaped flowerbeds

bounded by trimmed lavender are planted with acanthuses and Spanish broom (*Spartium juncium*), which is especially appreciated by perfumiers. Then there are bushes of Rose de Provins (*Rosa gallica* var. *officinalis*); this rose was originally brought back from the Holy Land by Thibault IV on his return from the Crusades.

The final two squares are kitchen gardens, each divided into two beds by central alleys. Here herbs and vegetables are cultivated: rosemary, thyme, sage, mint, parsley, beetroots, cabbages, carrots and pumpkins.

The promenade continues towards the pond, in which one can see the reflection of the château. A path crosses over the bridges and winds towards an elegant pavilion built in the same style as the arbours that look onto the water. From here you return towards the château.

In June the scented plants are at the height of their beauty: roses, lavender, broom, jasmine and aromatic plants waft their delicious perfumes. And this theme continues inside the château, which, rather appropriately, houses an exhibition on the history of perfumes from the time of the Renaissance.

The gardens at Chamerolles are beautiful throughout the year. In winter, when they are pure, bare and highly cared for, the architecture of the plants can be seen clearly. The colours, often softened by a layer of mist, are a range of greens and greys, with a few touches of dark red – a perfect match with the brickwork of the château walls. At Chamerolles everything is in harmony.

ABOVE *The impressive Château de Chamerolles built in the sixteenth century.*

OPPOSITE LEFT *The decorative and ornamental gates guarding the original entrance.*

OPPOSITE RIGHT *A mirror like reflection of the château in the water.*

TOP FAR LEFT *The château viewed through a carpet of cowslips (Primula veris).*

BOTTOM FAR LEFT *Water winds its way through the woodland in early spring.*

LEFT *The château is seen from across the lake through an arbour with dogwoods (Cornus alba) on either side.*

ABOVE *View over the yew maze.*

RIGHT *Stone obelisk surrounded by clipped box hedging.*

FAR RIGHT *Decorative detail from the stone obelisk.*

FAR LEFT TOP *The large bower bordering the Renaissance Garden covered in honeysuckle and roses.*

FAR LEFT BOTTOM *Detail of roses.*

ABOVE *An amazing series of clipped archways making an impressive avenue of hornbeams.*

CENTRE *The view across the lake in summer showing a 'Water Mirror'.*

CHANTELOUP
La pagode de Chanteloup

PHOTOGRAPHY BY DEREK ST ROMAINE AND LIZ EDDISON

 "This powerful and efficient man had an unusual quality. He could put his genius and vitality at the service of what was least useful and most fleeting: dedicating himself entirely to the perfection of an aria by Rameau, spending a fortune on installing appliances to circulate scents and water in the park. I believe that he placed charm above goodness, glory and wealth. Clearly he did not choose. The idea of depriving himself was horrifying to him. He wanted everything." This is how Madame de Choiseul describes her husband in Laurence Cossé's book *La femme du premier ministre.*

The Duc de Choiseul, to whom we owe the pagoda at Chanteloup, was a surprising man. And the pagoda itself is a surprising construction, an architectural jewel that takes us back into the magnificence of history. It stands erect, continuing to resist the ravages of time under the management of Thierry André, its owner and protector. Sadly, the pagoda is all that remains of the superb Anglo-Chinese gardens of Chanteloup.

In 1711, the Princess des Ursins invited the architect Jean d'Aubigny to build the château at Chanteloup and to lay out the gardens around it. She wanted the gardens to be in the French style with parterres de broderie, pools, a kitchen garden on the west side and staggered rows of arbours on the east side.

The Duc de Choiseul, as head of the government under Louis XV, exercised his power in order to purchase Chanteloup in 1761. By 1770 he was disgraced and exiled to Chanteloup, where he spent his time receiving and entertaining the famous and talented people of the era.

His additions to the château included domed pavilions, an orangery, a chapel, stables, and a series of courtyards, all of which were extremely refined and richly adorned with stone balustrades, string courses, dormer windows, statues, niches, low reliefs, pediments, porticoes, consoles and colonnades.

The Duke also had the gardens transformed by the architect Denis Le Camus to incorporate pathways laid out to offer views into the forest, a crescent-shaped body of water dug out as an extension of the Grand Canal, an Italian-style waterfall between the château and the crescent-shaped pool, and a formal kitchen garden. He also had the arbours on the east side re-landscaped to change them into an Anglo-Chinese garden, a very fashionable feature at the time, with pavilions, artificial grottoes, an ice-house and winding streams leading into waterfalls. As well as all this, a 12km-long aqueduct, part of which was underground, was constructed to join the Etangs des Jumeaux in the Forest of Amboise to the large pool. The difference in height between the two was only six metres, so the aqueduct had an almost imperceptible gradient.

To pay tribute to his illustrious visitors, he had a pagoda built at the middle point on the long side of the crescent lake as a vertical response to the horizontality of the lake. Le Camus took his cue from the pagoda built at Kew in 1757 by Sir William Chambers for the Princess of Wales, which was itself inspired by the pagoda in Nankin; Le Camus was also influenced by the pagoda in Canton. Though it has to be said that the pagoda at Chanteloup, with its crowning golden globe – a Chinese symbol of harmony – is far more elegant.

Whereas the Chinese built theirs in wood, at Chanteloup the pagoda is constructed using the local, very crumbly tufa stone. Its six floors are supported by a peristyle of sixteen columns. An internal stone staircase with a wrought iron ramp leads to the first floor, which houses a pink and white marble salon. The remainder of the staircase is in mahogany. From the top floor a fine view is offered over the countryside as far as Tours as well as a vista of the property's magnificent gardens. Inside, the pagoda is decorated according to the fashion of the Louis XVI period: acanthus leaves, pinecones and laurel crowns are carved into the pale stone that was taken from the site of the demolished Château de La Bourdaisière close by.

Thierry André explains that the duke furnished it with "sofas, tables, stools and armchairs in Chinese style, designed especially for the construction and arranged on each floor set into the geography of the building … Like the pagoda in Nankin, small lights and wind chimes were hung on the balconies to add the final exotic touch to this oriental building conceived for festive occasions."

The pagoda's slender outline and the details of its ornaments evoke the magnificence and elegance of times past. We can imagine the well-proportioned gardens created on an ambitious scale.

After the Duc de Choiseul's death in 1785, a few years before the Revolution, the estate was plundered and dismantled, leaving only the pagoda, the crescent lake, and the radiating avenues in the Forest of Amboise. There are seven avenues, just as there are seven steps leading up to the seven-floored Pagoda – seven was believed to be the number of perfection.

In 1910 René Édouard André, the son of the famous landscape architect and botanist Édouard André, saved the pagoda from ruin. "My grandfather later took up large-scale works," recounts Thierry André, "as the pagoda was built on wooden piles, like cathedrals. While the lake was full the building survived as wood soaked in water will last for ever, but the lake dried up. It was therefore necessary to dig beneath the pagoda and replace the wood with concrete, which was a very daring plan for the time, but it saved the building."

Since then the André family has made it their goal to preserve the Pagoda and the water in which it is reflected. To help us imagine the splendour of the past, the plans of the garden may be viewed in a pavilion in pure Louis XVI style at the entrance.

RIGHT *The Pagoda viewed from a jetty across the lake.*

ABOVE *The Pagoda showing all seven levels.*

RIGHT *A rowing boat on the lake.*

CENTRE AND OPPOSITE RIGHT *The interior of the Pagoda showing the staircases as they get increasingly steeper.*

LA CHATONNIÈRE
Jardins du château de La Chatonnière

PHOTOGRAPHY BY LIZ EDDISON AND DEREK ST ROMAINE

 As the American novelist Edith Wharton wrote, "The Italian garden does not exist for its flowers, its flowers exist for it; they are a late and infrequent adjunct to its beauties, a parenthetical grace counting only as one more touch in the general effect of enchantment." (Introduction to *Italian Villas and their Gardens*.) She might well have been referring to La Chatonnière. After all, Béatrice de Andia, the creator of the gardens, and Edith Wharton both lived in Saint-Brice near Paris, and La Chatonnière was indeed planned as an Italian garden. And yet La Chatonnière is a paradise for flowers.

Several things attract one's attention at La Chatonnière. Above all, its position: the château, its towers and gardens lie hidden, disguised and protected, like a happy surprise, at the end of a country road on the way out of Azay-le-Rideau in the district of Tours. Also remarkable are the power and intensity

of thought that Béatrice de Andia has put into its planning. In the same way that the gardens of the Italian Renaissance were designed to dialogue with the architecture of the Renaissance *palazzo*, the gardens at La Chatonnière were designed to harmonise with the valley of Touraine; cypresses, apertures, vantage points, overhangs, terraces, surprising effects, vases, urns, cut or dressed trees, topiary, and elaborately shaped flowerbeds all feature here.

The many species of perennials and shrubs are colourful, resplendent and varied. Like a brightly coloured carpet, every section boasts an intricately designed composition. Perfumed and in flower in every season, there is a sense of femininity in the gardens. Soft, rounded shapes prevail: the long Pergola des Fragrances is curved, the contours of the Feuille de l'Abondance are sinuous, the pools are round, and the maze is circular – even those gardens that are square, include a circular motif. This

roundness echoes the round corner towers of the house.

At this Loire valley château, whose history dates back to the Hundred Years War, its eleven gardens are laid out like a fan.

The green carpets of the Jardin de l'Elégance are brought to order by two intersecting paths that meet at a sundial. They are laid out to give views towards the distant horizons. Urns and mounted stone vases, built onto a low wall, and cone-shaped yew run the length of one side of the perimeter. A path rises towards undergrowth carpeted with white and pink cyclamens of Naples; of surprising beauty in the autumn, these plants lie beneath the large conifers shorn of their lower branches.

Higher up the valley, the path passes above the château and looks down upon the Jardin du Silence, which is based on the gardens of the Abbaye de Fontevraud. Featuring several cypresses, it takes the form of a large rectangle, which is divided into six green squares by lines of box that enclose two 'vases royaux'.

Next, one enters the Jardin des Fragrances, in which a long, semicircular pergola is dressed with a multitude of gold and yellow roses, including the two remontant varieties "Phyllis Bide", with its apricot-coloured double flowers tinted with pink gathered in bouquets, and "Mermaid", with its simple, large yellow flowers and golden stamens.

Openings in the sides of the pergola look out onto the Jardin de l'Exubérance – an expanse of hand-sown cornflowers, poppies,

and camomile – and, on the other side, onto the Jardin de l'Abondance – a beautifully manicured kitchen garden laid out elegantly in the shape of a rose leaf. Paths follow the patterns of the leaf veins, pushing their way into the precisely designed beds of fruit, vegetables, and aromatic and seasoning plants. Strawberries, aubergines, cabbages, cardoons, peppers and lettuce, flanked by basil, mint, vervain and chives, occupy their respective beds.

The Jardin des Sciences is set higher than the Jardin de l'Intelligence, which in turn looks down on the Jardin des Sens, the logic being that it is intelligence that allows us to enter the world of science but at the same time is supposed to control the senses. The composition of the Jardin des Sciences responds to the medieval nature of the château. Taking its form from a chessboard – a typical feature of medieval miniatures – it is composed of alternating squares of lawn and medicinal plants: thyme, artemisias, rue, digitalis, mallow, sage and rosemary, all scrupulously observing the borders of their squares.

The Jardin de l'Intelligence is well organised into four squares, like red and blue carpets: the red consisting of *Geranium sanguineum*, acaenas, centauries and carnations, and the blue of nepetas, lavender and bellflowers. All are set around a circular pool and closed by two pergolas of roses (including 'Madame Isaac Péreire' and 'Pierre de Ronsard') and clematis ('Lasurstern' and 'General Sikorsky'). It looks down onto the Jardin des Sens where small

and large squares gather round a circular pool. The five senses are kept alert by a symphony of perennials with generous blooms crowned by 'Alba Meillandecor' roses mounted on columns. In summer, these create a veritable white cloud above the bulb plants and the lilies, irises, peonies, perfumed lavender, gentle caressing grasses, bright blue or pink geraniums, pale yellow phlomis, asters and sedums, all of which bloom in profusion.

The Jardin des Romances has thirty round green chambers formed by living, dressed osiers that ring the garden and a circular yew maze. "Everything romantic is labyrinthine!" Béatrice de Andia likes to say. The domes of the osier chambers are coiffed with roses, each more lovely than the next, such as the charming pearly 'Madame Alfred Carrière', and 'Rose Marie Viaud', with its little purplish pink flowers. These are followed by gazebos, archways and cupolas, from where the gaze falls naturally on the chessboard or the pergolas of roses and honeysuckle.

Two new, freshly planted gardens are just taking their first steps: Les Luxuriances, which abounds with English roses from David Austen, and L'Invraisemblance (Garden of Improbability), where one can sit and admire the full cascade of gardens. This is a sight not to be missed!

Perhaps the best appreciation of the design and composition of the eleven gardens is had by the doves that live and flutter above La Chatonnière. To get such a good view of how it has all been so gracefully and skilfully woven together, we would need to hire a balloon!

ABOVE *Variegated* Miscanthus sinensis, *geraniums and alstroemeria in the Jardin des Sens. The last rays of evening sun turn the château an apricot pink.*

LEFT *The kitchen garden laid out in the shape of a leaf using pathways and* Buxus sempervirens *(box) as low hedges enclosing beds of different vegetables.*

OPPOSITE TOP LEFT *A view of the Jardin des Sciences.*

OPPOSITE LEFT *Pergola walk with roses and wisteria.*

OPPOSITE BOTTOM LEFT *A rustic pergola in the Jardin de l' Intelligence winds its way around the hillside covered in roses.*

TOP *Evening sunlight silhouettes the greenhouse.*

ABOVE *Pergola walk covered in roses.*

LEFT Salvia sylvestris, *roses, variegated miscanthus, geraniums and other perennials in the Jardin des Sens.*

ABOVE *Conical shaped yews* (Taxus baccata) *line a terrace adorned with stone urns and ornaments in the Jardin de l' Elégance.*

FAR LEFT *A living willow framework covered in yellow roses with a view of the herb garden in the Jardin des Sciences.*

MIDDLE *Millions of orange and yellow roses line the hillside in a crescent of fragrance.*

LEFT *Field poppies* (Papaver rhoeas).

TOP *A view through the Jardin de l' Intelligence showing the terracing.*

ABOVE *A view over the Jardin des Sens to the Jardin de l' Elégance.*

RIGHT *A circular bed of lavender and a carpet of campanulas and nepeta in The Jardin de l' Intelligence.*

CHAUMONT-SUR-LOIRE
Domaine régional de Chaumont-sur-Loire

PHOTOGRAPHY BY GARY ROGERS, LIZ EDDISON AND DEREK ST ROMAINE

 Innovatory, daring, ingenious, extravagant, unusual, imaginative, novel, provocative… in the Chaumont Festival all the gardens, which are designed by landscape gardeners from around the world, have been created to stimulate ideas. But Chaumont is not just the Festival. It is an historic place, with a château, outbuildings and stables, a park, and an exhibition space for contemporary art. In short, a medley of nature and culture.

Chantal Colleu-Dumond has been the new director of the Domaine Régional de Chaumont-sur-Loire since the start of 2008 and it is her goal to make this combination the hallmark of the domain. As she points out, Chaumont is the only château built on a panoramic viewing point over this undeveloped section of the Loire. The site is magnificent and unequalled. Amboise and Saumur, to which Chaumont can be compared, are both encircled by a village, but here the château reigns supreme on a site by the river's edge, which is otherwise untouched.

Medieval but embellished by the Renaissance, the château has opened its doors to many famous men and women throughout its history: Catherine de Médicis and Diane de Poitiers during the Renaissance, Madame de Staël in the early 1800s, and Prince and Princess de Broglie later in the nineteenth century.

The park underwent extensive alteration during the nineteenth century. As we learn from Corinne Larsabal, who studied the château in depth for her university dissertation, little remains to allow us to imagine how it was before the work undertaken by Henri Duchêne in 1880.

The property had been purchased in 1874 by Mademoiselle Marie-Charlotte Say, a sugar heiress, who became Princesse de Broglie by marriage. She and her husband introduced luxury and magnificence to Chaumont and revitalised the park.

They invited one of the great landscape gardeners of the period, Henri Duchêne, father of the famous Achille, to transform the park. On his arrival he found a large avenue leading to the château, a promenade lined with linden trees overlooking the Loire, a large kitchen garden that ran alongside the main avenue, flowerbeds close to the château, and vast lawns lying all around.

He proposed two plans and the Prince decided on the one in which the kitchen garden was to be moved to make landscaping effects possible. Duchêne redesigned and replanted the park to create a garden in irregular style as was the fashion of the period, that is to say, an English-style composition imbued with a French spirit. It was given sweeping, at times circular, avenues and copses of trees of a single species, whether deciduous or evergreen, such as maple, oak, beech, pine, cedar and sequoia. And vast lawns were laid down to expand the views onto the château and landscape. The result was very close to the park seen today.

After admiring the coppices of large trees and touring the château and stables that offer an understanding of the history of the place and the spirit that guided its creations and renovations, you should visit the gardens whose perimeter was designed by the Belgian landscape gardener Jacques Wirtz at the start of the 1990s. Then, pay tribute to Jean-Paul Pigeat, the founder of the Garden Festival at Chaumont; with his innovative idea he breathed new life into this sleepy castle and its park.

Next, pass over a bridge decorated with false tree trunks in the Rocaille style, which was popular in the nineteenth century, view the rockery that boasts a surprising collection of ferns, stop in front of the Vallon des Brumes (Valley of Mist) planted with collections of shade plants from Japan, where, as its name suggests, a mysterious dampening mist floats.

And, finally, pay a visit to the new gardens. Hedges of beech trace out the shape of a large leaf and thirty smaller 'leaves', each of which encloses a more or less trapezoid garden. Covering an area of about 250 square metres, each small garden has a different aspect, quality of soil and level.

Every year the Festival has a different theme, such as 'Crisis' (1993), 'Acclimatisation' (1994), and 'Mobiles' (2007); in 2008 the theme is 'Gardens for Sharing'. What is shared in a garden? Cuttings and seeds of course, but also secrets and *savoir-faire*.

Each garden is supposed to be a source of new ideas as well as a workshop. Each décor is composed of perennials, shrubs, bulb plants, and above all annuals. The best gardens are awarded prizes and some of them are kept until the following year. The qualities most sought by the members of the jury are imagination and originality.

This is a wonderful learning opportunity for visitors: how to deal with annuals, make unusual combinations of perennials, use the light to create effects of colour, choose a hedge, an ornament, a gazebo or a tunnel, use water to supply fountains and waterfalls, discover new techniques with the use of new materials … all of which are presented according to ecological principles.

Chantal Colleu-Dumond hopes that the recent introduction of an artistic programme, entitled 'Arts and Nature' – a topic dear to her heart – will enrich the theme of the garden and carry it into the future.

RIGHT *500 painted pots arranged in the garden are controlled by the visitors as they are moved. Planted with ophiopogon, nigrescens, festuca, helianthemum and echinocactus.*

TOP *Carpet bedding in tribute to the town of Blois, which was well known for its superb floral displays. Garden designed Nathalie Bernard.*

ABOVE *A pebble mosaic.*

RIGHT *Visitors at the entrance to the India Song Garden, part of the 'Colours of India' Festival (1999), with the turrets of the château of Chaumont-sur-Loire behind. Garden designed by Patrick Blanc and Eric Ossart.*

TOP *The courtyard is made up of restored farm buildings belonging to the château and is planted differently every year. It is seen here in September.*

LEFT *A September border including* Miscanthus sinensis, *phormiums and salvia.*

ABOVE *One year 'Carpet Bedding' was the theme for the Festival. This giant turtle is made up of many different plants including helichrysum,* Perilla frutescens, *thyme, alchemilla and artemisia.*

ABOVE *Linen drying in the wind is the inspiration of this garden, entitled Wind and Sails, which was designed by Sonia Gros and Sonia Keravel. The cloth acts as a hammock or swing.*

TOP RIGHT *A boardwalk designed by Mathilde Lenglet to celebrate the memory of Brazilian landscape designer Roberto Burle-Marx.*

RIGHT *A wooden bench and sculpture of a gardener standing in the shade of a tree. Garden designed by Gerhard Höepfner and Pepinières Bruns.*

CENTRE *The Garden of the Blue Trees. These tree branches (painted blue) appear to be going for a walk. Garden designed by Christine O' Loughlin, Catherine Villefranque, and Michel Euvé.*

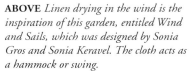

ABOVE *A yellow panel from Just Move It, a garden made up of moveable sliding panels and planted wooden boxes. It was designed by Laurence Di Meo, Benoit Allemand and Emmaneulle Floch.*

LEFT Pennisetum alopecuroides.

CHENONCEAU
Parc du château de Chenonceau

PHOTOGRAPHY BY NICOLA STOCKEN TOMKINS

On 20 September 2002 the Jardin Vert at Chenonceau was the setting for the official naming of the rose 'Dames de Chenonceau'. Created by Delbard, it is modern but with the appeal of an ancient rose: a double bloom with an attractive furl of pink petals with hints of apricot. Its name summarises the history of the château, which has nearly always been ruled by women, sometimes even queens.

The foremost of these great ladies was Diane de Poitiers. A favourite of King Henri II, who gave her Chenonceau, she adorned the property with an enchanting sunken garden that seems to have been built on the waves. And her influence is still felt. As Alain Roger, the head gardener, who with all his talent and care looks after the gardens so well, says: "*Chez* Diane, we plant 32,000 flowers each year," as

though she were still here, a regular visitor who strolls around the garden paths! But in a way she *will* always been here, reigning over the Jardin de Diane.

On the King's death, his queen, Catherine de Médicis, took back Chenonceau and in exchange offered her Chaumont. To erase Diane's power, which she had clearly always resented, Catherine created her own garden in pure Renaissance style influenced by Italy. She turned the Jardin de Diane into a kitchen garden and orchard planted with the best species and varieties of the age. "In the Jardin de Catherine we plant 12,000 flowers each year," Alain Roger continues. Catherine, it seems, is also still present in her gardens, though the ornamentation she installed has disappeared.

The next lady to take up residence at Chenonceau was Madame Dupin, wife of the financier Claude Dupin, who held a salon there and received, among others, philosophy and literary giant Jean-Jacques Rousseau. In the nineteenth century Madame Pelouze undertook to restore Chenonceau and its gardens with all their Renaissance spirit. These latter 'Dames de Chenonceau' were perhaps less brilliant than their predecessors, but were just as attached to the château and its park. They would have done anything to protect it.

Today, the principal avenue, lined with two very lovely rows of plane trees, crosses the moat and continues through the French-style

gardens bordered by a narrow path. Great care is taken over the lawns: the grass is first cut using a rotary mower, then by a mower with a spiral blade, giving the effect of an English lawn. Majestic cedars of Lebanon lend further elegance to the scene.

The Renaissance façade of the château is preceded by the Tour des Marques, a vestige of the Middle Ages, complete with arrow slits. These wonderful buildings are surrounded by water. The château extends on a bridge built over the River Cher by Diane de Poitiers and is heightened by a gallery added by Catherine de Médicis where the queen used to hold brilliant parties.

The Jardin de Catherine lies below a keep, the Donjon des Marques. It was designed originally to be a typically Renaissance "garden of curiosities", with an aviary, menagerie, sheepfold and artificial grotto standing alongside square flowerbeds. The garden lies between the château and the Jardin Vert (created in the nineteenth century) where, on the far side of the orangery, there stands a very beautiful holm oak. The old stables nearby feature a clock-tower from which a carillon plays out its tune, calling time to order.

The floral compositions in the Jardin de Catherine are very intricate and refined. The plants have to like rain but they have to like drought too. In spring tulips, forget-me-nots, wallflowers, pansies and crowds of lavender bloom here. In May everything is pulled up

and verbena, ageratum and sage are planted around the existing tree roses. The colours and compositions are altered each year.

Passing in front of the château takes us back to the Jardin de Diane, which was designed for Diane de Poitiers by Italian architects. The garden is divided by paths into eight grassy triangles where santolinas form grey arabesques against the green of the lawn, and at the centre of the garden stands a fountain. The beds are planted with blue, pink and mauve hibiscuses, which are almost one hundred years old. Built after the flood of May 1940, the surrounding terrace protects the garden from flooding if the river rises. It has the effect of making this sunken garden seem to float on the water.

In the woods, close to the avenue of plane trees, there stands a yew maze. This labyrinth, typical of Renaissance gardens, is circular; at its centre, a small iroko gazebo provides support to a jasmine. On the far side of the maze stand four caryatids representing Greek figures. In the time of Catherine de Médicis they adorned the façade of the château, but were moved to their current location by Madame Pelouze.

On the other side of the avenue of plane trees you will find the kitchen garden. It is laid out formally with square beds of flowers and vegetables and is divided by paths that meet at a pool. Columnar yews mark the intersections of the paths and the entire perimeter of the garden is lined with cordon espaliers of apple trees that are as pretty in flower as their fruit is tasty.

The kitchen garden is particularly lovely in spring when its innumerable tulips of all colours are in bloom; chosen from early and late flowering varieties, they are cultivated in beds like the vegetables. The château's florist, Marjolaine Vaucelles, includes the tulips in the many flower arrangements that she creates to adorn the rooms of the château. It is pleasant to watch her work in her flower studio in the sixteenth-century farm next to the kitchen garden. Her compositions make use of Roses de Noël, narcissi, violets, cyclamens, leeks, delphiniums, dahlias, eremurus, peonies, asters, amaranths and sunflowers. She works in concert with the gardeners and all the rooms in the château, from the kitchens to the chapel, are adorned with fresh flowers twice a week.

Chenonceau and its 'floating' gardens are where nobility, magnificence, grace and refinement reign uncontested.

RIGHT *The château creates a dramatic backdrop to the Jardin de Diane, a sunken parterre in which hundreds of metres of santolina hedging twist and curve over the lawns.*

OPPOSITE RIGHT *Curving path showing topiary domes of yew with box and euonymus in the Jardin de Diane.*

OPPOSITE LEFT *The sixteenth-century Château de Chenonceau spans the River Cher.*

ABOVE *The Jardin de Diane, a formal parterre with straight gravel paths edged in topiary and colourful beds of gaura, begonia and standard hibiscus.*

RIGHT *In the potager, an ornamental birdcage is suspended from an arch.*

MIDDLE *In the potager, Black-eyed Susan (Rudbeckia fulgida) scrambles up cane wigwams alongside rows of celosia.*

OPPOSITE TOP *Alain Roger, head gardener at Chenonceau, standing in the potager where he has worked for all his adult life.*

OPPOSITE BOTTOM *The potager, a medley of fruit, vegetables, herbs and flowers arranged in beds.*

CELOSIE

TOP *A huge, ancient Indian bean tree (*Catalpa bignonioides*) towers above the path leading to the Jardin de Catherine.*

LEFT *The Jardin de Catherine, a formal parterre beside the River Cher. A central fountain is surrounded by four quadrant beds filled with the standard rose 'The Fairy'.*

ABOVE *A wooden pergola raised on ancient stone columns is clothed in fragrant white star jasmine (*Trachelospermum jasminoides*).*

TOP *In the potager, the old sixteenth-century farm building creates a calming foil to rows of spring tulips.*

ABOVE *By mid spring, the potager is filled with row upon row of brightly-coloured tulips.*

MIDDLE *Les Domes and the Chancellerie are seen across the Jardin de Diane, a sunken formal parterre.*

OPPOSITE TOP *Ancient doorways are glimpsed beneath the emerging leafy canopy of a small chestnut grove.*

OPPOSITE BOTTOM *In the centre of the Jardin de Diane, a tall, slender contemporary fountain plays, whilst spirals of tightly-clipped low santolina hedging play across the lawns.*

CHEVERNY
Parc et jardin de Cheverny

PHOTOGRAPHY BY DEREK ST ROMAINE AND LIZ EDDISON

The Château de Cheverny is encircled by green lawns and a landscaped park incised with riding avenues. Though for many years the château was renowned for its hunting tradition, hunting is no longer practised in the park; today, the hounds, horses and roe deer co-exist peacefully in their green surroundings.

The main axis of the gardens starts at the orangery, traverses the château and the French gardens, proceeds along the Allée d'Honneur, passes through the gates into an avenue lined with cedars, and then links with the long, sinuous procession of flowers, the "serpentine fleurie".

This classic, noble and stately setting has been enhanced by the Marquis de Vibraye's touch of imagination and modernity.

The château is a living, rather than inhabited, residence. At its centre stands an entrance pavilion flanked on either side by pavilions with tall, sloping, French-style roofs. At the sides are two towers with domed roofs, each crowned by a viewing gallery. The south façade of the château opens onto an expanse of lawn, while a flight of steps from the north façade leads to the new gardens.

The outbuildings feature a footbath and a dovecot dating from the eleventh century and restored in the sixteenth. Behind the outbuildings you will be attracted by an enclosed garden filled with flowers, scents and colours; this is the kitchen garden. It is divided into rectangular beds, some of which are hedged in by low lines of box that separate the flowers – pansies, lilies of the Incas, hardy geraniums, 'Iceberg' roses and dahlias – from the vegetables, including cabbages, artichokes, leeks and cardoons. Exuberant hops are supported by frames, and a square bed planted with berry bushes makes a pair with a square bed of vines. Some of the paths are lined with apple trees.

The kitchen garden adjoins the kennels where the hounds of the Cheverny Hunt live. The sixty or so dogs – a cross between English foxhounds and French poitevins – exercise in the park.

The grounds at Cheverny resemble a forest, with large numbers of majestic trees: there are poplars, Corsican pine (*Pinus nigra maritima*), Scots pine (*Pinus sylvestris*), sequoias, and bald cypresses (*Taxodium distichum*). The latter, which live with their roots in the water, turn superb colours in autumn. There are two water-courses in the park: the Courpin is a small stream that runs into a large body of water, and the Conon is a small river that flows through the estate.

On the way back towards the château, the path leads towards the orangery and the new gardens.

Simple and classic in design, the orangery dates from the eighteenth century. Five large rectangular windows line the building on either side of the central triangular pediment, and its slate roofs match those of the château. Traditionally, the orange and citrus trees would be grown in pots, stored in the orangery during the rigours of winter, then taken out during the warm weather to adorn the French gardens.

Today the orangery looks onto the green chambers and winding serpentine of flowers in the Jardin Contemporain. This garden was the idea of the Marquis de Vibraye, the design of landscape artist Magali Fuchs, and the creation of young apprentices who have found their vocation working on this project.

The marquis wanted nothing to obstruct the views between the orangery and the château, and also wanted water to feature in

the new design. The composition Magali Fuchs presented retains the geometry of traditional gardens and the colours of English gardens. It is contemporary in its manner of reinterpreting the two styles and integrating a serpentine of flowers that disrupts the established order, flowing through the garden like a stream that at moments one loses sight of, before it then reappears.

Viewed from the first floor of the château, the garden's overall arrangement becomes clear. It is formed by several chambers of plants that follow the length of the main axis. In the first parterre, the trimmed yews in the French gardens are replaced by conical apple trees.

Lines of blue perovskias converge on the main axis, and the serpentine grows out of this in a winding path of lavenders.

The Salle des Pommiers is geometric but also asymmetrical. It is planted with 'Everest' *Malus*, whose beauty shines twice a year: in flower in April, and in fruit in autumn. The serpentine continues its course with saffron-coloured 'Paprika' achilleas, bright red 'Lucifer' *Crocosmia latifolia,* and warm-coloured grasses.

The Salle du Bassin is rectangular with a small fountain at its centre. The serpentine, which halts at the pool, starts up again in tonalities of orange, blue and violet. Your gaze is drawn through the gaps between the hornbeam, or through the openings in the fences of woven living willow, and towards the periphery of the park and its majestic trees, particularly the cedars.

The third chamber of the serpentine, as it nears the orangery, is represented by the pergola. Its curved frame echoes the domed roofs of the château and its bowers are heavy with wisteria and clematis. At their feet, perennials and bulb plants cheer the seasons: tulips, alliums, digitalis, irises, fennel and sedum blend joyously. There are also cotinus, acanthus and abelias, which are all very lovely in the late summer.

The serpentine cuts through the pergola and then makes its last curve as it crosses the lawn before finally rejoining the far end of the large main axis around which the park is ordered.

ABOVE *A rectangular pool and fountain leads the way down from the château towards the orangery.*

OPPOSITE LEFT *Alstroemeria, used as cut flowers in the château, make a colourful display in the potager.*

OPPOSITE RIGHT *A border of pink and white dahlias and ornamental grasses including* Miscanthus sinensis *and* Stipa tenuissima *in the potager.*

ABOVE *The imposing formal entrance facade to the Château de Cheverny.*

RIGHT *A gardener cutting flowers for cut displays within the château.*

FAR RIGHT *A wooden bench placed underneath the pergola.*

OPPOSITE *The contemporary design of the pergola lined with Sedum spectabile combines well with the pool, fountain and facade of the château.*

TOP *Swamp cypress in the River Canon which runs through the estate.*

ABOVE *A living willow hurdle bridges the gap between hornbeam hedges.*

RIGHT *Vegetables and flowers grow happily together in the potager.*

OPPOSITE TOP LEFT *A couple of metalwork chairs surrounded by dahlias in the potager.*

OPPOSITE BOTTOM LEFT Parthenocissus *(Boston Ivy) covers a water tower.*

OPPOSITE RIGHT *A plantation of poplar trees grown for timber in the extensive woodland near the canal.*

DRULON
Jardins de Drulon

PHOTOGRAPHY BY GARY ROGERS AND DEREK HARRIS

 "A flower for each day of the year". That could be the slogan at Drulon, where a moment does not pass in which a bud does not open: roses, peonies, herbaceous and climbing plants, bulbs, and flowering shrubs fill the place to profusion.

The current owners, Piet Hendricks and his wife, were immediately taken by this property. They felt that Drulon was the ideal place to realise their long-held dream of creating a flower garden as a setting for displaying contemporary art. The work was hard at the start as the ground had been invaded by bramble bushes and ivy had overrun the buildings. They even had to chop it out from inside the château. But it was worth it, now art works – most of which are changed on an annual basis – are placed along the paths, well integrated into the garden, which is filled with an abundance of flowers throughout the seasons.

In winter there is always a bulb or shrub opening up a corolla and unfurling some stamens – a viburnum, a honeysuckle or a camellia – even though the winters are as severe as the summers are hot and dry.

Spring begins with the narcissi, and the white flowers of *pyrus* trees grouped close to the outbuildings. These are followed by the quince trees that create a very beautiful orchard at the entrance (and they are just as impressive in autumn when they are in fruit). The pinkish-white flowers of the nashis (*Pyrus pyrifolia*), which line the crossed paths in the old kitchen garden, are equally charming. These small fruit trees originated in the Far East and are the result of the crossbreeding of a pear tree and an apple tree by the Japanese. They give crunchy, juicy and very tasty fruits that are much loved by the bees.

Every summer there is a flower festival held in the Jardin Floral and the Jardin de Paeon when the peonies comes into spectacular bloom.

The autumn blazes in all its glory with the coming of the dahlias, asters and reflowering roses, some of which bloom until Christmas.

The history of the château goes back to the fifteenth century, as indicated by the arrow slit in the tower, but its construction was continued in the seventeenth century. In times past, the lords of the manor lived here fully self-sufficient, and evidence of this can still be seen around the estate: its barn and grain lofts, pigeon house, fishpond, stables, cowshed, pigsty, bread oven and orangery.

Visitors should start their walk in the Jardin Floral, next to the Cour d'Honneur close to the house. It is enclosed as it was originally the old kitchen garden. It has always been a dream of Piet's to surround himself with an excess of flowers whose beauty and colours he can share with his wife and visitors. "Pleasure is always greater if it is shared," he says.

In his design of the flower garden, Piet followed the advice of Alix de Saint-Venant and Jacques Gérard. Composed of rectangular beds, it is crisscrossed by paths, with the two main paths meeting at a round pool at the centre. In addition the garden is crossed and enclosed by a long pergola. Interestingly, the colours are grouped in bands, passing from cool through to warm tones: green and white; mauve, pink and blue; pink and red; and, finally, yellow and orange.

The Jardin Floral is in flower from mid-April to late December. Irises, hemerocallises, grasses, asters, Japanese anemones and dahlias growing in the mulch-covered earth are accompanied by clematis and roses – bushes and climbers, ancient and modern, botanic, natural and English. The green and whites include the rose 'Sally Holmes', the green rose *Rosa viridiflora*, the 'Whirlwind' Japanese anemone, white poppies (*Papaver orientalis* 'Perry's White'), *Rosa rugosa* 'Blanc Double de Coubert', the hibiscus 'Diana', Sweet cicely (*Myrrhis odorata*) with its fern-like foliage, plus phlox, delphiniums and galegas.

In the Jardin des Chambres the vegetation creates ringed enclosures of shadberries, hydrangeas and hibiscus amongst which stand sculptures separated from one another by the flowers. A pond at the centre is surrounded by a theatre of greenery.

Passing by the Jardin des Fougères, where the profusion of ferns is very green and luxuriant, brings you to the lake, where everything is refreshing and peaceful, and where two swans glide serenely by.

Returning towards the château by the Allée des Davidias, the mood changes once again, quickly returning from the wild to the sophisticated. It is worth taking a moment to pause in the Jardin du Château, where you will find the fishpond and its surface of white waterlilies.

From here, carry on to the Secret Garden, with its pigeon house, small buildings roofed with flat tiles, an old gardening workshop, the bread oven, and the cellar where works of art are on show. It is a cool, walled garden featuring azaleas, maples, ferns and hydrangeas, including *Hydrangea paniculata* 'Pink Diamond' and *H. villosa*.

Next comes the Jardin de Bacchus, planted with fifteen different sorts of vine. And, finally, the Jardin de Paeon, which, as its name suggests, is dedicated to peonies. The tree peonies come into flower at the start of May, followed by the herbaceous peonies, which remain in flower until mid-June. Their blooms are spectacular and Piet has planted several hundred of them.

RIGHT *The entrance to the Jardin Floral under the blossom-laden branches of an old cherry tree.*

ABOVE *The beautiful* Iris sibirica *which features in many parts of the garden of Drulon.*

OPPOSITE TOP LEFT *Border with berberis, hibiscus, perovskia and crocosmia.*

OPPOSITE LEFT BOTTOM *Border of* Phlox paniculata *and dahlias in the Jardin Floral.*

LEFT *The Jardin de Paeon with borders of* Iris sibirica, *peonies, English roses and grasses.*

115

RIGHT *Summer border in the Jardin Floral with hollyhocks, roses, monarda and Verbena bonariensis.*

BELOW *'Ready for Takeoff' by the artist Karel Zijlstra.*

BOTTOM *'The Rotor' by the artist Pieter Obels on a barn wall.*

TOP *A border in the Jardin Floral including* Aster novae-angliae.

ABOVE Rosa *'Maigold'.*

RIGHT *A selection of the many grasses at Drulon with hollyhocks and phlox.*

FAR RIGHT *Hollyhocks* (Alcea rosea) *in the courtyard.*

ABOVE *Borders of* Iris Sibirica, *peonies (*P. suffruticosa *and* P. rockii*) and the hedge plant berberis in the Jardin de Paeon.*

FAR LEFT *The sculpture 'Flowers' by the artist Imara Reuling in the Jardine des Chambres with* Iris Sibirica *in the foreground.*

MIDDLE *One of the many interesting groups of grasses in the Jardin de Paeon with grasimelus, miscanthus, and cocosmia.*

LEFT *The sculpture 'Lauke Mate' by the artist Karel Zijlstra in the Jardin Floral.*

LA FOSSE
Parc botanique de La Fosse

PHOTOGRAPHY BY GARY ROGERS AND DEREK HARRIS

The trees seem bigger, more generous than elsewhere. The grass underfoot, like a mossy carpet, is strewn with white 'handkerchiefs' dropped carelessly by a *Davidia involucrata*. A forest of wild rhododendrons (*Rhododendron ponticum*) and other species colonises the undergrowth; in May the plateau is almost completely mauve. A shrubby peony forming a dome loses its yellow petals and all around Turk's-cap lilies are reseeding themselves.

Images like these make the botanical park of La Fosse exceptional. It is a very elegant, radiant place, if only because of the ambitions of the members of the Gérard family, who have looked after it and unfailingly developed it,

generation after generation. Its collections have ensured that it is registered as one of France's Historic Monuments, a place of reference.

It is Jacques Gérard, the park's owner and protector, who set up the Associations des Parcs et Jardins en Région Centre, which he has directed for several years. As he explains, he was just following in the family tradition: "One of my ancestors was one of the founders of the Société Nationale d'Horticulture de France, and my father, Philippe Gérard, was also a founding member of the Association des Parcs Botaniques de France in the 1970s. This, with the Journées des Plantes de Courson, brought about a renewal in the gardening world in France."

Jacques Gérard goes on to describe how the present park came in to being: "The first exotic plants to be cultivated here began in the eighteenth century around the house that was built in the sixteenth and enlarged in the seventeenth. At the start of the nineteenth century the park was landscaped on the other side of the buildings by Alexandre-Sébastien Gérard. He had studied at the École Polytechnique and in those times that meant that he had also received a solid education in artistic matters, particularly architecture. He laid out the park in the fashion of the time, that is to say that he created a wooded park as opposed to an open one. That is why today the park so closely resembles a wood. The period when most new plants were introduced

was between 1890 and 1939, as a result of the opening up of Asia, and consequently the Asian plants have become acclimatised. Large numbers of American plants were also introduced. The dogwood plants, some of which are Asian, others American, amazed our ancestors."

"In 1900 my grandfather set up a phenomenal hydraulic system that could haul water a distance of 1800 metres, up a rise of 60 metres, to fill an enormous reservoir of 1000 cubic metres, allowing him to water all the plants. This explains how this place can be a botanic garden. Thanks to this watering system he was able to keep young plants alive even though they were set on a dry hillside in the full sunshine. He also created an ornamental lake. Right from the start, there has always been a member of the family ready to continue the work begun by our forefathers."

"They liked to try everything," he continues, "beautiful and interesting plants, rarities. Like everywhere, they had successes and setbacks, and everything was done purely from a sense of aesthetics, without a care for classification. That is why the trees and shrubs are planted like enormous flowerbeds."

"In winter, it is all tranquil. In spring the white blossom is astounding: the prunus, magnolias, exochordas, dogwood and viburnums are in flower. Fritillaries, scillas, columbines and orchids naturalise themselves in the underbrush. In autumn the carpet of

Neapolitan cyclamens remains amazing until the first frosts. In summer the foliages on the trees reaches maturity."

The park is shaped like a triangle. A sorbus-lined avenue starts at the entrance and divides the park into two parts. On one side, a hillside descends towards the Loire; on the other, a plateau lies on the boundary between Perche and Touraine. At its beginning, the avenue is bordered by very beautiful shrubs, peonies *Itea ilicifolia*, viburnums and osmanthus grow freely or are trimmed. On either side huge beds are planted with large conifers, strawberry trees, dogwoods, giant heathers, cedars of Lebanon and magnolias, such as the rare *Magnolia ashei*, with its spectacular leaves and flowers.

The avenue climbs further and enters a glade called La Pièce d'Eau. It is a garden within a garden, inhabited by ferns and hellebores, and cut through by small winding paths that lead

you from one surprise to another. This is where you will find the famous *Davidia involucrata*, only the second example of its kind to be introduced into France. An old lake with an island and a bridge is a reminder of the park of Les Buttes Chaumont.

Nearby, the Allée des Écorces features trees with remarkable barks: *Prunus maackii*, *Prunus serrula*, *Acer griseum* and *Betula albo sinensis* vie with one another for originality.

Faithful to the aesthetic principles of the park, another clearing follows a denser section of wood. Crossing the large avenue to the slope that runs down from the plateau, one finds rhododendrons have invaded the ground beneath the indigenous trees, offering a panorama of lovely mauve flowers.

The path leads to the Belvédère, which is crowned by a pigeon house. It is a very elegant building with a small round room and colonnades. The outer perimeter is lined with vases from Anduze where, in summer, perfumed pelargoniums are grown. "Here, we are in Italy," notes Jacques Gérard. And indeed, looking around you will see holm oaks and even an umbrella pine.

The Parc Botanique de La Fosse has always been cherished by knowledgeable nature-lovers. Jacques Gérard is happy to associate the joys of botany with charitable work. A part of the entrance ticket fee is donated to *Vaincre la Mucoviscidose*, the association fighting cystic fibrosis.

ABOVE *In early spring the park offers interesting vistas of the trees to visitors walking on the moss covered paths.*

OPPOSITE LEFT *A view from the entrance pathway over the buxus toparies, towards the castle.*

OPPOSITE RIGHT *The striking Belvédère, which is crowned by a pigeon house.*

ABOVE *The castle viewed under the* Cedrus libani *(Ceder of lebanon).*

LEFT *One finds many surprises amongst the trees, such as this* Hydrangea paniculata.

RIGHT Camellia sasanqua, *which flowers in October.*

OPPOSITE RIGHT *The magnificent* Cedrus libani *planted in 1810.*

OPPOSITE *In autumn the floor of the woods are covered with a carpet of Cyclamen de Naples.*

MIDDLE *One of the highest paths in the park, leading to the Belvédère with its dovecote.*

LEFT *View from the dovecote over the ever-changing countryside.*

BELOW *The upper corner of the 'Promenade' in early autumn featuring acers, pinus and prunus.*

125

LE GRAND COURTOISEAU
Les jardins du Grand Courtoiseau

PHOTOGRAPHY BY DEREK HARRIS

 As is commonly known, Christopher Lloyd wrote the column *In My Garden* in the magazine *Country Life* for years. It was a pleasure to read every week. On one particular day, he exclaimed, "I plant to please myself!" This phrase could have been the maxim of the creators of the Grand Courtoiseau gardens.

These gardens have been fashioned by lovers of beauty, by sophisticated gardeners who have indulged their own tastes without worrying whether they are 'good' or 'bad'. The Grand Courtoiseau represents their personal preferences, with no compromises.

It is a peaceful garden, where tranquillity reigns, where there is no conflict, everything is fluid, and the gentle colours are set against a naturally green background to soothe the eye.

The estate dates back to the fourteenth century and remained in the same family for five hundred years. The present manor-house was built in the seventeenth century. It is a very lovely property, with tall, brown-tiled mansard roofs, a flint base, warm-coloured roughcast, and brick dressing. The building comes complete with an enclosed courtyard, a harness room, and its own chapel. The house has welcomed many a well-known name through its portals, including the politicians Clémenceau, Jean Jaurès, and Aristide Briand. More recently, the writer Hervé Bazin lived here. As the President of the Académie Goncourt he would receive many writers including François Nourissier, Jean d'Ormesson, Michel Tournier, and Michel de Saint-Pierre, as well as journalist and creator of *Le Figaro Magazine*, Louis Pauwels.

It is around the elegant manor-house that Jean-Hervé Dussordet – along with his sister and brother-in-law, Monique and Guy Herdhebaut – has composed the garden. They started work on the project in 1991. Initially, they set about searching for archival materials, but the lack of available information encouraged them to throw themselves into a purely creative project.

Why this garden? Why does anyone create a garden? Monique, Guy and Jean-Hervé reply: "We were born in a garden. We grew up with it. It trained our eye. We were obliged to leave it but we missed it. We wanted to return to what we had known. This is a condition for which there is no remedy!"

"So we went from garden to garden. From nursery to nursery. From gardener to gardener. And we tried to interpret all these experiences… We attended seminaries lasting several days at Vasterival, the property belonging to Princess Sturdza, near Dieppe. We owe her a lot. We would spend the day there and in twenty-four hours we could learn as much as twenty books could teach us. We have tried to remain as faithful as possible to what she taught us."

"Fifteen years ago we were doing the spadework. That is all done. Now we scratch at the surface and carry the kitchen peelings down to the garden. We make our own compost. This mulch nourishes the ground. The worms aerate it. The soil is soft. The mulch allows us to save on water. It smothers weeds and halves the amount of weeding required. Princess Sturdza taught us the most rewarding and easy steps to take. Those that are physically and financially least demanding, and which give the greatest returns".

What gardens have they been influenced by? "All of them," comes the reply. "If they have a soul. Even if they are only three metres square. There are always scenes that inspire you, always things to learn, which you absorb in your own manner."

What is a garden with a soul? Jean-Hervé Dussordet explains: "It is a garden behind whose appearance there lie pairs of hands, innumerable footsteps and a gaze!"

A visit to Yvoire made a big impression, the trio explain: "It was just taking shape, it was actually coming into being, but already it was possible to appreciate the structure Alain Richert had created. That visit stimulated us to contact him. We had already designed the garden but we wanted to show him our plans. We talked a lot. He spent a day here. He then submitted a plan of his own that placed a different emphasis on the structures we had proposed, while also offering his own ideas. We adopted his plan."

"The creation of a garden is fascinating because it is a never-ending job. Your appreciation becomes keener, you always want to make improvements, you make constant progress. And behind any garden, it should never be forgotten that there are human beings, knowledge and a love of gardening."

The elegance of the manor is echoed by a very fine hedge of yew, which immediately sets the tone. These green walls are interspersed by pillars topped by hemispheres, all in yew, creating natural sculptures that unify the manor-house and the gardens, setting both off to best effect. Moreover, the traditional forms of the topiaries emphasise the exuberance of the plantations, and the dense, dark green of the yew brings out the colours of the flowers.

The yellow-flowered nasturtium (*Tropaeolum tuberosum*) – as seen in the gardens of Scotland or at Powys Castle in Wales – climbs on the yew walls. The red-flowered nasturtium is more delicate, needing humidity and a gentle climate, but here the winters can be cold and the summers dry. "We have tried eight times," Jean-Hervé Dussordet notes smilingly. In gardening you must never give up!

The tour begins in the Jardin du Faune, a green chamber enclosed by walls of yew in which the main axis offers a long perspective that takes in a pool and fountain and, at the far end, a sundial. The view is divided into compartments on either side by more yew hedges; yellow, pink and blue flowers are planted inside each compartment. Shrubs, perennials, ancient and English roses offer their colours and scents from Easter right through to All Saints Day. The first chamber is a garden of ancient roses in which the two entrances are adorned by squares of lavender.

The ancient ditches have been planted and organised in a remarkable fashion. In the Jardin Italien, Alain Richert has designed a series of diamond-shaped pools that flow from one into another, starting from a mural with a fountain, where the water gushes into a basin. The pools are surrounded by a profusion of perennials that mostly prefer shade and humidity: gunneras, euphorbias, Japanese irises, rodgersias, astilbes, ligularias, ferns and hostas. The embankments on either side are planted with azaleas, mahonias and spindle-trees.

To reach the pendant to the Jardin Italien, you have to pass by the winter garden and in front of the manor-house; the façade of the house, which looks onto the park planted with rare trees, is dressed with a line of hemerocallis and very lovely japonicas in orange-tree boxes that bloom in spring and bear spectacular yellow fruit.

You pass into the Jardin Exotique, which is a tribute to Augustin Cornu de la Fontaine de Coincy, who once lived at Le Grand Courtoiseau. He was a botanist who cultivated, amongst other things, pineapples in the very beautiful winter garden. An abundance of bamboos, hydrangeas, viburnums, polygonums and other plants originally from distant corners of the world leads to his charming glasshouse in which today all sorts of cuttings are prepared.

On one side, the Sous-Bois aux Essences offers a winding walk through the trees, some chosen for their attractive bark, planted with selected hydrangeas and camellias.

You pass through the Jardin des Érables Japonais (Garden of Japanese Maple) – delicate and transparent in spring, flamboyant in autumn – to reach the Jardin des Antiques,

where the grassy expanse is cut to different lengths to create a vast circular design with intersections and paths that cross diagonally or at right angles. This lovely green space is decorated with statues, basins and sculptures, and is planted at the centre with a copse of sorb trees from Tibet.

On the other side of the Allée des Tilleuls (Avenue of Limes) – planted in the seventeenth century as the principal entrance to the manor – lies the Jardin des Fruitiers. This orchard is planted with different varieties of apple, pear and plum trees and is reached by an avenue lined with magnolias that, like the fruit trees, bloom in spring.

This delightful promenade, in which the impression is given that nothing has been left to chance, leads back to another era, when one still took time to listen to the singing of the birds, perhaps. For this, of course, is what the name of the gardens refers to; Le Grand Courtoiseau used to be called La Cour des Oisons. And the birds are still here.

ABOVE *The historic manor house adorned in May with a wonderful display of* Wisteria sinensis.

ABOVE *The ripe quince in the courtyard with autumn colours.*

RIGHT *Detail of* Cydonia oblonga *(quince).*

LEFT *The courtyard in spring with flowering quince planted in containers.*

BELOW *The majestic lion guarding the Jardin du Faune.*

BOTTOM *Looking down on the ornamental pond in the courtyard garden.*

ABOVE *View through the Jardin Italien in early spring with rodgersia, astilbes, ligularias, hostas and ferns.*

LEFT *A spring view of the Jardin du Faune with the pond and fountain surrounded by trimmed yew walls.*

TOP RIGHT *Entrance to the 'Species Underwood', a wooded area with gunnera and hydrangeas.*

RIGHT *The Jardin Italien with its decorative fountain and planted with hostas, gunnera and astilbes.*

LEFT *A corner of the Jardin du Faune with autumn coloured* Cornus florida, *rubra, alstroemeria and asters.*

RIGHT *Bamboo* (Phyllostachys viridis).

FAR RIGHT *The magnificent Avenue of Limes, planted in the seventeenth century, on a misty autumn morning.*

BELOW *The entrance to the Jardin Exotique with a display of containers with hostas, hydrandgeas and a view through to the bamboos.*

LES GRANDES BRUYÈRES
Arboretum des Grandes Bruyères

PHOTOGRAPHY BY DEREK HARRIS

It is amazing to think that the superb gardens of Les Grandes Bruyères were all inspired by just a single pot plant brought back from England. Today, the magnolias and cornus collections are recognised by the Conservatoire des Collections Végétales Spécialisées.

A love of plants, nature, beauty and elegance, a thirst for work well done, and an enjoyment taken in the effort required to maintain this very demanding park on a daily basis have led Monsieur and Madame de la Rochefoucauld to create this botanic garden, where heathers (notoriousy difficult) are in their element – as the name of the arboretum indicates (bruyères = heather).

This vegetal, wood-scented universe blends into the Orléanaise forest. All the plants chosen harmonise happily with the Scotch firs that were already growing here and which give them their protection. Their colours complement one another: the greens, whites and pinks are in marvellous unison. "It is as though they were members of an orchestra in which each plays its own score," Brigitte de la Rochefoucauld likes to say.

When she does something, she does it properly. If she breeds wirehaired fox terriers, she raises champions and studs. When it comes to plants, furnished with the best advice, whether it be from Princess Sturdza, the Princess de Chimay, or Jelena de Belder, Madame de la Rochefoucauld produces

collections that become points of reference.

As for Bernard de la Rochefoucauld, he is busy becoming a great specialist on heathers in France in record time. He visits the most famous heather gardens, meets experts, makes his selections, orders, plants, and propagates, and even writes authoritative books on the subject. *La Bruyère* is a compendium that is at once dense, practical and of great clarity. It includes the colour chart drawn up by the British Heather Society: amethyst, crimson, magenta and lilac, all of which are represented in his park.

It all began in the 1970s. "We built this dream house in the middle of the forest for lack of space in Paris with five children," Brigitte de la Rochefoucauld relates. "We began by clearing a meadow around the house, which in summer dried yellow like a doormat. One day, on a trip to England, we saw a sign saying 'Heather Nursery'. I, as a painter, was enchanted by the endless colourations of their leaves and flowers, so we bought a pot and planted it. Bernard propagated some and we began to market them. They sold very well. At that time we were advised by the Vicomte de Noailles and the Princess de Chimay, whose gardens filled us with wonder. 'You have to start from the house, deal with a room and then continue outside,' they told us. We were also helped by some landscape gardeners. Tobie Loup de Viane designed the courtyard. And Russell Page made a memorable visit here; he was very harsh,

but everything that he said happened just as he predicted."

"Winter 1985-86 was terrible," Bernard de la Rochefoucauld continues. "The temperature went down to minus 25. For ten days it was below -20, something that had not happened since the time of Louis XIV. We nearly lost everything. The heather collection migrated to Monsieur Dauguet's."

"But we did not give up and introduced new specimens unceasingly. This winter we planted 5,000 heathers and 340 trees. There are 6,000 specimens labelled. We have created new settings, such as pools of water at a bend in the grassy path, similar to the ponds of the Sologne."

You enter through a structured garden set flat on a terrace. Taking its cue from French gardens, it has patterns of box enclosing lavender and heather. There are large quantities of lavender and heather, which serve as an introduction to the pink ocean of the park. A pergola in the shape of a cross is draped with roses and clematis, and there is a pool at the centre.

To reach the wild, though managed, garden that spreads around the house one must descend a few steps buttressed by bushes of yew. The house stands as though in the middle of a vast clearing. Its walls are lined with the marvellous roses 'Albéric Barbier' and 'Gloire de Dijon', trained branch by branch, and two very lovely wisteria, one mauve and the other

pink. The lawn is of exceptional quality: "à l'anglaise", it sets everything off marvellously.

Behind a first beech hedge, which acts as a sort of boundary, the undergrowth garden begins under the cover of the Scotch firs, which give shade to the beds as far as the eye can see. Grassed paths wind between between ground-covering or arborescent heathers, magnolias and perennials like sedums and thalictrums. Self-sown scillas grow all around, as well as the lovely green-flowered plant *Smyrnium perfoliatum*.

Through a second, tri-coloured beech hedge is the arboretum. First come the 'Collines Chinoises' (Chinese hills) flecked with heathers, and pools of water bordered by seas of hostas and primroses, then passing from clearing to clearing one reaches the American arboretum. The deeper you enter the arboretum, the wilder it becomes. This is where Bernard and Brigitte de la Rochefoucauld attempt to acclimatise the new varieties arriving from around the world, most of them in the form of seeds. In this sandy, rather acidic soil, they have built a national collection of magnolias and a registered collection of cornus. There are also collections of *Acer*, *Pinus*, *Quercus* and *Stuartia*, each specimen carefully labelled with its name, its origin, provenance and the year it was planted.

And then there are remarkable trees, like an immense common oak (*Quercus robur*), which must be more than 250 years old. It stands

in the middle of a clearing where it receives abundant nourishment in spring, which it absorbs in record time. One of the rules of the arboretum is to give each plant water and food individually, which explains why they are in such good health and so magnificent.

The heathers are to be found everywhere and bloom throughout the year. During winter the alpine heathers (*Erica carnea*) are in flower, as in their natural habitat, their blooms arriving when the snow melts. *Erica darleyensis* flowers in April and May, at the same time as *E. erigera*

and the arborescent heathers – the perfumed *E. arborea* that is seen in Porquerolles, and *E. australis*, both of which form marvellous bushes here. In June the delicate 'Daboecia' appear with their small white or purple bells that last until the first frosts. Other varieties that will bloom all summer are *Erica cinerea* and *E. vegans*. Finally, *Calluna vulgaris* comes out between August and November, with its greatest moment in September when it sets the beds aflame with colour.

You return to the house to find the Maze

where, between the hornbeam hedges, very beautiful ancient roses are grown for their perfume: Brigitte de la Rochefoucauld's favourites are 'Cuisse de Nymphe Emue', 'Duchesse de Montebello', and 'La Petite Orléanaise'. "This collection was built up at the end of the 1970s with André Eve," she explains, "who shared my passion for ancient roses at a time when you could only see them at l'Haye-les-Roses."

A little further on, a traditionally laid out kitchen garden with sections separated by

flat-cut yew provides the house with food, all without the use of any chemicals. Indeed, none of the plants in the Arboretum des Grandes Bruyères receive any chemical treatment, which is why this place is a haven for insects and birds. Everything here is planned with the greatest respect for nature and beauty.

ABOVE *Early morning autumn mist around the pines and heathers in the peaceful 'Arboretum Chinois'.*

RIGHT *The De Vos and Kosar Magnolia 'Pinkie'.*

MIDDLE *The Allee Le Men in early autumn with changing leaves, heathers, box, pines and cornus in flower making a peaceful and tranquil scene.*

FAR RIGHT TOP *The 'Secret Garden' in spring with heathers, clipped box hedging and topiary in a wonderful display of green.*

FAR RIGHT BOTTOM *The Stele Le Guennec with a stream full of ferns and primulas wandering around large beds of flowering hostas in summer.*

BELOW *Detail of a border with acanthus and phlox.*

ABOVE AND RIGHT *At the top of the arboretum is the Etang d'Edmond with trees (maples and pines) showing autumn colours.*

OPPOSITE LEFT TOP *The wonderful old oak* (Quercus), *the centrepiece of the Jardin de Sous-Bois, in spring colour.*

OPPOSITE LEFT BOTTOM *The imposing Allee de la Princesse de Chimay in spring with blossoms and heathers.*

OPPOSITE FAR RIGHT *The Allee de la Princesse de Chimay, this time displaying the peaceful colours of summer.*

LA MARTINIÈRE
Arboretum de La Martinière
PHOTOGRAPHY BY DEREK HARRIS

The Arboretum de La Martinière is a sanctuary. It is a place of silence and peace where nature imposes its laws in full freedom. The only sounds one hears are birdsong, the flapping of wings, rustling, the sounds of impalpable, subtle, living things: poetical nature. The only sights are mist and haze, slanting sunlight, sunsets, ripples on the breeze-blown surface of the water, the movements of the fish, silhouettes, boughs, foliage, flowers, fruits, bark and even mushrooms. It is a wild garden.

If nature is the protagonist, Michel Davo is its director: he creates settings like paintings – whether seen from afar or close up – in their smallest detail. Nothing escapes him. A streaked bark, a stamen, a stalk – there is nothing that does not have a meaning for him. And his awareness of nature is as great on a small scale as it is when it comes to creating large, scenic effects.

Everything here seems natural, and yet most of the trees and shrubs were planted only forty or so years ago. It all began in 1967, when Michel Davo inherited what was then a rather unprepossessing place: little more than a sandpit, where the rather acidic soil had been laid bare by bulldozers. He let it be; kept quiet; waited and watched.

"Pioneer plants began to take hold spontaneously", he explains. It was not long before a prairie had created itself, "daisies, wild carrots, willowherb, grasses and nettles arrived". All these plants either cohabited or struggled to survive. The spectacle is unending. There is always something happening. The wild carrots sow themselves, mature, run to seed, are covered by rime, and then by snow. They are lovely at any time of the year, whether tender and promising, or mature and withered; you only have to take the trouble to look at them.

If he knows how to appreciate the plants, it is because Michel Davo is an artist; he creates mobiles. Often made of bamboo, they are fascinating, especially when he makes them float on the pond. "Works of art?" asks Sylvie Roux. "Certainly they are works of art, but ephemeral and changing; they live, flaunt themselves, die and are reborn to the rhythm of nature, and in accordance with the atmosphere of the moment."

Michel's gardening knowledge comes from his observations, his exchanges, his extensive reading, and his numerous journeys. He has visited Thailand, China and Brazil several times.

On our arrival, a pine with a round top provides an appealing, Mediterranean touch to the setting. It is a *Pinus densiflora* 'Umbraculifera', a small, slow-growing tree whose silhouette is reminiscent of umbrella pines.

A barrier has been built between the two ponds. Rising in tiers on either side are shrubs with arched branches, either climbing or crawling dwarf conifers, *Picea pungens* 'Nana', *Juniperus virginiana* 'Grey Owl', sprawling spiraea shrubs, dwarf laurels, *Prunus laurocerasus* 'Otto Luyken', the more imposing golden yew, *Taxus baccata* 'Standishii', and a *Miscanthus sinensis* 'Zebrinus'.

The path takes us to some land lying fallow and to Michel Davo's house, which is made entirely of wood – telegraph poles to be exact! The path then leads us past one of his artworks, which he calls *Un Tableau Composteur*. Here, layer upon layer, he has piles of leaves, cabbages, apples, bananas, bark and pine needles. The different 'strata' are clearly visible in profile through a glass pane. This playful tableau stands surrounded by wild grasses.

What method does he use in his gardening? "This place planted itself, or I lent it a hand", he explains. "I guide nature. Some things grow well, others not. There is nothing rational here, nothing sophisticated. I progress in small touches, as my inspiration takes me." He does not use fertiliser, just the mulch created from crushed waste, but it brings outstanding effects. For example, the ground bark of *Alnus glutinosa* gives a lovely orange mulch. It was a simple thing to do. His freedom of spirit, artist's imagination and the liberty he gives to nature combine to bring about extraordinary discoveries. He dares, it is as simple as that – and the barriers come tumbling down. If there is a storm or drought, he doesn't persist, he just takes note and remains philosophical.

He allows things to take their own path to such a degree that he has allowed a wisteria (*Wisteria chinensis*) to overgrow some fallen trees. It is dynamic! "It creeps and, when it finds a support, it climbs," he notes. And it has become gigantic, filling the entire end of the first pond and straddling several giant trees. When it is in flower, it is simply spectacular.

Like every daring gardener, Michel Davo does not hesitate to introduce plants that

would not normally be at home in this setting. They have an exotic and amusing aspect and, in the end, adapt very well. Thus you pass by plants from the south, like rockrose, *Cistus purpureus* and white-flowered *C. aguilarii*, nandinas, *Eucalyptus parvifolia* and *E. niphophila*, which have withstood temperatures of –15°C, a mimosa *Asacia dealbata*, yuccas, pistachios, and even a palm, *Trachycarpus fortunei*, which he saw in Yunnan, umbrella pines, and strawberry trees, *Arbutus unedo*, which reseed themselves bountifully, and *Arbutus arachnoïdes*, with its beautiful reddish trunk.

Michel Davo is very familiar with bamboos. He has a hundred or so species and varieties. Each one has an exceptional characteristic: *Phyllostachys nigra* 'Boryana' has a marbled thatch, *P. edulis* produces tasty shoots, *P. nigra* sends out black canes, *Chimono-bambusa* quadrangularis has square foliage, and in Touraine *Phyllostachys* edulis and *P. viridiglaucescens* can grow to a height of 15 metres.

What are his favourite bamboos? *Chimonobambusa tumidissnoda* with its prominent knots like cymbals and slender leaves, and its elegant and supple fanlike bearing, and *Phyllostachys iridescens* with leaves streaked with different greens and trunks that reach 7cm diameter in the Arboretum.

The bamboos, which are generally very difficult plants to assimilate, are perfectly integrated in this wild garden. Here they can achieve their full splendour and natural physical development. They have been planted in colonies that are echoed by the waterside plants growing in family groups: horsetail, *Equisetum`americanum,* with its evergreen ribbed stem, and grasses, *Zizania aquatica*, whose foliage is very evident in winter even when it withers and takes on pretty, soft, sandy colours, similar to the ribbon-like leaves of the bamboos.

Water plays an important role in this garden,

and is in constant movement. Michel Davo's mobiles, like small, light sailing boats, follow the movement of the wind across the surface, edging their way through the aquatic plants: white water lilies, lotus, *Nelumbium*, a tiny floating fern named *Azolla caroliniana*, aquatic carnivorous bladderworts, *Utricularia vulgaris,* and, at the water's edge, willows lean over and rest on the surface. In autumn, the colourful fronds of the liquidambars and maples emerge above the morning mists that sometimes float on the ponds: it is a very special moment.

It is all very peaceful. The only sounds are the bustling of the mallards on the water, the blue splash of a kingfisher, or the sweeping tails of the Koï carp. Silence imposes itself naturally on the place and induces meditation and contemplation. But the most serene moment of all comes at the summer solstice, when the sun sets along the length of the pond – magical.

ABOVE *The natural pondside with silver birch, maples, pines and bullrushes in autumn colours.*

LEFT *The larger of the two pools with floating mobiles by the artists Michel Davo and Didier Ferment.*

TOP *Throughout the garden you will find interesting constructions by Michel Davo.*

ABOVE 'Un Tableau Composteur', *the fascinating picture by Michel using garden and domestic 'waste'.*

RIGHT *Amazing growth of this bamboo* Phyllostachys viridiglaucescens *with Michel Davo showing the scale after a few months.*

FAR LEFT *Autumn colours reflected in the still tranquil pond and showing the wild and natural look of La Martinière.*

ABOVE *The bamboo* Chimonobambusa tumidissinoda *in the arboretum.*

LEFT *The leaf of the exotic* Trachycarpus fortunei.

FAR LEFT TOP *The variegated leaves of the bamboo* Arundinaria auricoma.

FAR LEFT BOTTOM *There are many hanging bamboo constructions by Michel Davo, making 'curtains' as you walk around the arboretum.*

LEFT *A symphony of trees and bamboos, including maples, in autumn colours giving a wonderful display.*

ABOVE *Close up of* Liriodendron sinensis *leaves.*

TOP *Close up of* Rhus chinensis *leaves in autumn.*

LE PLESSIS SASNIÈRES
Jardin du Plessis Sasnières

PHOTOGRAPHY BY GARY ROGERS AND DEREK HARRIS

A plateau. A country road that descends into a valley. A church. An avenue lined with poplars – and all the scents of the best of England. You have arrived at Sasnières.

Subtle thought has gone into this garden's creation: a certain conception of beauty, elegance and nature. And not just thought: extensive knowledge, long experience, a mastery of techniques, and time. After all, a garden is not made in a day, it requires a far-reaching vision. This is the "art des jardins."

Rosamée Henrion's knowledge and experience of gardening are legendary; she is the reference. If you don't know the name of a plant, or you don't know the difference between a *boulingrin and a vertugadin, ask Rosamée

Henrion, she will tell you.

Rosamée Henrion and her son Guillaume are the heart and soul of this garden. "I was lucky enough to spend time with the friends of my mother who loved plants and were also aesthetes," she says. "The Princess de Chimay had written a treatise on the art of gardens entitled *Plaisirs des Jardins*. The Viscount of Noailles had a garden in Grasse. And the Duchess de Mouchy and his 'Potager' were famous. My uncle, Emilio Terry, had designed the follies at Groussay." These high society amateur gardeners forged Rosamée Henrion's taste.

At Sasnières she began to plant the area close to the house, then, bit by bit, to spread across the rest of the park. Guillaume, an interior decorator, "wanted more precision" she says, so he gave the overall plan a structure. He traced out the hedgerows, straightened others, introduced topiaries and designed patterns for the box. He has many projects, though naturally some are overtaken as new inspiration strikes.

"We never set down a preliminary plan," Guillaume explains, "but went ahead as the fancy took us." Everything was composed consistent with a deep and sincere admiration for the "English" approach, beginning with a high degree of refinement and that particular intimacy with plants that is typically British: "Treat plants respectfully, they are people!" as Valerie Finnis used to say.

The result is a multitude of themes with those all-important details. The garden appears characterised by intuition, but its apparent freedom is underpinned by well-concealed control: staged settings in which flowers are always coming into bloom as others lose theirs, plants that reseed themselves, topiary forms, mixed borders, divisions in yew between different sections of the mixed borders, a finely worked gate at the entrance to the old kitchen garden, well nourished and healthy perennials, large trees, rare plants, densely planted beds, and carefully manicured lawns.

"My mother inherited this place in 1960," Guillaume Henrion tells us. "Its history goes back to the fifteenth and sixteenth centuries but we have no documentation for it. The house has been uninhabited since 1914. There used to be a large area of fallow land around it. It was very romantic, with trees everywhere and a pond in the middle."

The tour begins past the mill made welcoming by its 'Sally Holmes' and 'Stanwell Perpetual' roses, bell-flowers and Japanese anemones. On the garden side, the mill looks onto some very elegant and well-cut yew topiaries that immediately set the tone.

The Allée des Sangliers is named for the two wild boar carved in stone at the start of the avenue. Sometimes the garden is visited by real boar, as well as by stags and roe deer! Scillas carpet the ground beneath the trees, and columbines, digitalis and euphorbias reseed

themselves at the feet of holm oaks, prunus and paulownias.

Climb up to the plateau and you will find a long avenue of shiny-leaved *Magnolia grandiflora*. In summer their strongly scented flowers diffuse their fruity perfume down towards the stream, the lake and the managed section of the property. Beyond that lie the church tower, the château, the outbuildings, the pond, and the flower garden. The avenue is closely mown and rollered, as is the English custom, to create a long green carpet that is soft to walk on. The forest was very densely planted in the period between 1914 and 1960, but Guillaume has now thinned out the vegetation and uprooted some trees to allow in more light.

You come out of the forest above the Jardin des Fleurs. The spectacle is magnificent. From here the layout of the garden, set in the ancient horseshoe-shaped kitchen garden enclosed by walls, is clearly visible. A pergola, also in the form of a horseshoe, follows the line of the perimeter.

The pergola provides support for very wide mixed borders interspersed with yew divisions that separate the sections planted with bulbs and perennials on the basis of colour. First come yellow and white, then blue and pink, yellow and bright red where the beds curve, and lastly dark purple, almost black. The plants include roses, peonies, asters, poppies, bell-flowers, delphiniums, nepetas, wild bergamots, penstemons and euphorbias against a background of shrubs like cotinus and buddleias that give volume and structure to the large compartments.

In the spring this garden is enchanting for the blossom of the apple trees along the arches of the pergola, which are mixed with large numbers of white hellebores and tulips. The flowers of the apple trees in question – the *Malus* 'Everest' – give small apples in autumn.

At the centre of the garden a path starts at the entrance to the old kitchen garden marked by a very attractive, finely wrought gate, then passes between the two rows of the pergola, and heads off towards the pond. On either side a very formal pattern in box, designed by Guillaume, has been cultivated on the grass. Green on green, in contrast to the multi-coloured flowerbeds. Two semi-circular beds, curving in opposite directions one after the other, are planted with Portuguese laurels cut in hemispheres above a bare trunk.

Next comes the kitchen garden – with its crops of vegetables, aromatic plants, nursery section and soft fruit – which, in turn, leads to the Shrubbery. Here Rosamée Henrion has brought together her favourite shrubs, including an exquisite deutzia *(Deutzia setchuenensis* var. *corymbiflora)* with delicate white blooms. The more common plants are set to the rear, to act as a backdrop emphasising the flowers and textures of the rarer plants in the foreground.

An opulent cryptomeria acts as a transition to the Jardin d'Eau where a stream, the Sasnières, falls in cascades and is lined with semi-aquatic plants such as rheums, gunneras, hostas and primroses *(Lysichitum americanum)* that stand with their feet almost in the water.

At the mill, which faces the Glacière, shrubs have been planted in tiers, and in spring ceanothes blanket the escarpment with their blue flowers. In April, as you approach the mill, the pink blooms of deciduous magnolias harmonise with similarly coloured tulips, which together blend with the brick of the building.

These impressionistic and uninhibited touches of colour are very charming and they are set off all the more by the dark forms of the yew topiary. This is what Sasnières is all about, it is a garden of contrasting feminine and masculine characteristics: flowers and precision.

*A *boulingrin* is the French word for a sunken grassy bed in which ornamental patterns are created by plants (the word was derived from the English 'bowling-green'). A *vertugadin* is an amphitheatre of terraced lawns.

ABOVE *The magic atmosphere of an early morning in late summer. A view from the hillside path looking west over the park.*

OPPOSITE LEFT *A section of the middle border with the apple arches,* Cotinus coggygria *and* Verbena bonariensis.

OPPOSITE RIGHT *Summer border with* Perovskia atriplicifolia.

ABOVE *Autumn colours across the spring-fed lake.*

BOTTOM LEFT *Detail of a border with kniphofia.*

BOTTOM RIGHT *Border in the east garden with crocosmias and daylillies, hemerocallis.*

MIDDLE *View to the château over colourful border of heleniums, crocosmias and* Echinacea purpurea.

FAR RIGHT TOP *Detail of* Echinacea purpurea.

FAR RIGHT BOTTOM *Border with perovskia and bubbleja looking towards the château.*

ABOVE *By the arch a group balls, cubes and cones made from box.*

LEFT *A view over the lake towards the village with beds of* Cleome spinosa *in the foreground.*

RIGHT *A carpet of hosta and* Cleome spinosa *under a grove of silver birch (*Betula utilis *var.* jacquemonti *'Doorenbos').*

FAR RIGHT TOP *Borders in the east garden featuring* Echinacea purpurea, Lagerstroemia indica *and* Buddleja davidii *('white cloud').*

FAR RIGHT BOTTOM *A late summer border in the east garden with asters, sedum and* Persicaria *'Darjeeling Red'.*

ABOVE *View across the lawn and lake to the château.*

TOP RIGHT *A section of the 'Cascades' with* Gunnera manicata *and* Lysichiton americanum *on the banks.*

RIGHT *A morning view over some of the eleven hectares of garden from the upper path, with fields of wild flowers including* Digitalis purpurea *in the foreground.*

FAR RIGHT *A peaceful corner by the lake on a late summer afternoon, taken from underneath the branches of an* Acer x zoeschense.

LES PRÉS DES CULANDS
Arboretum des Prés des Culands

PHOTOGRAPHY BY DEREK HARRIS

Imagine a peaceful, refreshing garden where water flows gently. The Arboretum des Prés des Culands is an unusual place cut into square plots by small canals. It is a garden of pure and simple passions where you can learn about the plants in the totality of their universe, whether botanic, horticultural or even symbolic.

Pierre Paris is a holly specialist, the mere mention of his name immediately conjures up the picture of holly. Though he is also devoted to maples, hostas, astilbes and hemerocallises, which love the same conditions, the holly remains his number one interest. In fact

his collection has been given the status of a Collection Nationale by the Conservatoire des Collections Végétales Spécialisées, and it has been recognised by the Holly Society of America. Today it contains about 60 species and 400 hybrids and cultivars.

The style of the Arboretum des Prés des Culands comes as a complete surprise – it certainly doesn't lack originality! The hollies and other plants stand on islands encircled by waterways known as 'Mauves'. This term refers to the slow-moving courses that run into the Loire with a small but regular flow. The water rarely freezes, its temperature remaining fairly constant at around 8 – 11°C (46.5° – 52°F), even in winter.

In the seventeenth century this marsh was a great garden with all its land under cultivation. One of its crops was hemp, which was used to make the sacks that transported the flour from the thirty-five mills that used to operate at Meung-sur-Loire. With technological progress, however, and the resulting abandonment of hydraulic power, the marsh, which had been cleared and put under cultivation by monks in the Middle Ages, lost its vocation and was soon taken over by nature once again.

Pierre and Nadine Paris bought up the plots of land in 1987 and at that time they were covered by willow, alder, ash and poplar trees. It was the ideal place to form a collection.

It was during a visit to the botanical garden in Dublin that Pierre Paris went into raptures while standing in front of a magnificent hedge of holly, a usage that was unknown in France. This observation spurred him to collect hollies to be able to study new uses for the plant. To do so he undertook a scientific approach by bringing together the greatest possible number of species and varieties so that he could observe their habit, foliage, flowers, fruits and hardiness.

Pierre Paris hopes that the hollies will be appreciated for their vigour, resistance to the cold and ease of cultivation – they like almost all kinds of soil and are happy in damp or dry ground, in the shade or the sun. He hopes that they will not be reduced to simply being thought of as trees or shrubs with glossy, persistent and prickly leaves, and pretty berries. For, as he points out, there are holly varieties whose leaves drop in winter, others whose leaves are not prickly (like *Ilex* 'Camelliifolia'), those that flower, and others whose fruits are not only red but orange, white, black or dark brown.

Some have a very particular habit, like the slender, sweeping and supple *Ilex castaneifolia*, one of the most beautiful in the arboretum. It has a real presence and elegance and, the specialist informs us, "is excellent as a windbreak".

Pierre Paris is painstaking in his studies of the plants: he notes their least stamen, the peduncle, he is aware of the colour of their wood, the slowness or rapidity of their growth, the spread of their branches, their overall shape (ball-like or pyramidal), the beauty of their green or bluish shoots, and how they develop through the seasons.

This passion has led him to exchange cuttings with gardens abroad, like Rosemoor in England, which holds a collection of holly recognised by the National Council for the Conservation of Plants and Gardens, the Bokrijk arboretum in Belgium, Wichita in the United States, Varel in Germany, and even the botanic garden in Shanghai.

Pierre Paris regularly creates new plots to extend his experimental laboratory. He digs out the ground, puts down a compost that he prepares himself, arranges the ground with care, and plants continually. The specimens he plants are of all sizes, ranging from simple shoots to mature shrubs.

The species he plants here on the islands grow spontaneously around the world. The hollies come from the Americas, China, Japan and Korea. He mixes them very naturally with narcissi, hart's tongue, royal osmund, periwinkles, cyclamens, primroses, hostas, hellebores, daphnes, mahonias, tree-climbing clematis, and astilbes, which are also very beautiful in winter as some of them have spectacular shapes, and he leaves them standing to dry until spring. These he combines with large numbers of aquatic or semi-aquatic plants such as ligulas, willows and skunk cabbage (*Lysichiton americanum*), and with the luxuriously leaved yellow spath (also known as Peace lilies) whose deep roots help to stabilise

the banks. The plants live in company with carp, ducks, bullfinches, various members of the tit family, greenfinches and even squirrels. At times it is also possible to see roe deer and coypu, which are both very fond of nibbling on leaves, roots and berries.

So, what is Pierre's favourite holly? He has no favourites, he loves them all, for him the choice of plant is influenced by its intended use. For example, for a hedge he recommends *Ilex* x *attenuata* 'Hossier Waif', a slow-growing tree that will grow between 6 and 9 metres (19ft 8in. - 29ft 6 in.) tall. If you want one without prickles, then use *Ilex cassine*, whose long smooth leaves are rounded at the ends. For groundcover, then *Ilex crenata* or *Ilex*

rugosa. If you wish for a fine-standing, isolated tree with a pyramidal shape, then choose *Ilex* x *koehneana*. For a tree with variegated leaves, try *Ilex altaclarensis* 'Nobilis Picta' with its creamy coloured edges. If you are in search of a deciduous holly, he would select *Ilex decidua*. And one with yellow berries? Then *Ilex aquifolium* 'Bacciflava'. There is a holly for every situation.

The Arboretum des Prés des Culands is beautiful all year round. In spring the perennials, trees and shrubs are readying themselves and their tender new shoots contrast with the dark, persistent foliage of the hollies; and the narcissi, periwinkles and daphnes are in flower. In summer, the astilbes,

hydrangeas and Japanese anemones are in full bloom. In autumn the colours of the holly berries accompany those of the maples, whose shimmering livery quivers above the water; this is a very lovely period. And the winter sets off the glossy foliage of the hollies, which glint in the slanting rays of the sunshine. The light is never hard here, and is always filtered by the large trees, even if they have lost their leaves. It is these reflections and sparkles that give the Arboretum des Prés des Culands its charm.

Pierre Paris is very pleased that hollies are becoming increasingly popular in private gardens. As he points out, they are good for people with very little space as they can even be grown in a pot on a terrace or in a courtyard,

like the fastigiated variety *Ilex aquifolium* 'Green Pillar'. And their docility allows them to be cut into topiary forms.

In this place carved by canals, suggestive of the Hortillonnages d'Amiens or the Marais de Bourges, Pierre Paris's impassioned work is bearing fruit and his original idea of popularising the holly in France gradually makes headway.

ABOVE *A colourful view of a waterway in spring lined with maples, rather like a green Venice.*

LEFT *Reflections of trees.*

ABOVE *The main waterway lined with maples and hollies.*

LEFT *A glorious collection of new spring colours on the bank of a small island in the middle of the garden.*

TOP, ABOVE, LEFT AND RIGHT *A wonderful medley of colours with the waterways, trees and plants giving a feeling of peace and tranquillity in this special place.*

TOP Ilex aquifolium cornuta *part of the Collection Nationale at Les Pres des Culands.*

ABOVE Ilex Aquifolium cornuta Burfordii *x* pernyi.

LE PRIEURÉ D'ORSAN
Jardins du Prieuré d'Orsan

PHOTOGRAPHY BY LIZ EDDISON AND DEREK ST ROMAINE

 Certain places, such as Le Prieuré d'Orsan, have an undeniable power. Perhaps it is the fervour of Robert d'Arbrissel, the founder of this medieval priory, still influencing the place centuries later? Or, perhaps, it is the dedication of Sonia Lesot and Patrice Taravella, who have worked so hard to create a garden typical of a medieval miniature.

In the middle of rough, unsophisticated Berry stands this self-contained property with a grove of silver poplar trees: enclosed, light and perfect. Enclosed like all medieval gardens; light because the excellence of its architecture, woodwork and plants reveal a mastery that achieves lightness; and perfect because of the evident harmony between the priory and its gardens.

It is a very beautiful place, but it is almost

as though this was a by-product, a happy accident. In fact, Patrice Taravella is not interested in beauty for beauty's sake. To him, beauty is just one result of the more important criterion of functionality. Function creates form, and beauty can only flow from that. "Ornamentation holds no appeal for me," he explains. For example: "The reason we have bird boxes here is not because we want bird boxes. It is so that the birds can nest here and play their role. So that they can work for us and eat the caterpillars."

"And the reason the Cloître de Verdure garden is harmonious is because it has to be peaceful, a place propitious to meditation. It is not square but the eye is persuaded that it is through the interplay of lines. From chaos I have engineered order, to soothe the spirit. I have developed sequences, played on filled and empty spaces and on high and lows. I have introduced regularity into zones of light and shade through the use of hornbeam bowers to slow the pace of our visitors and invite them to silence."

"Here we have a garden of medicinal plants but it is not the plants that interest me. It is their utility that fascinates me. Why is a lungwort called by that name? It's not by chance! There are relationships between plants and man that I find really exciting," he continues.

You have to visit Orsan with these ideas in mind. Nothing is unplanned here, it is all

carefully thought out, both in principle and in the smallest detail, then put into practice by the enormously talented gardener Gilles Guillot. Distances are carefully calculated, the plants have a symbolic value, and the materials are chosen with care. The techniques used have been studied in depth and tested. And it should be emphasised that Patrice Taravella insists that every gardener also knows how to cook; the relationship between the gardens and the kitchens at Le Prieuré d' Orsan, where the cuisine is renowned, is very strong.

The tour begins with the medicinal plants in the garden called Les Simples. This immediately brings to mind the atmosphere of a medieval monastic garden. Four square beds lined with woven branches lie alongside the outbuildings, the walls of which are lined with espaliered fruit trees. The plants, all local and labelled, were used to cure the sick, as healing was one of the duties of a monk.

The main path leads to the left to the Cloître de Verdure. This is a square garden lined with arbours of hornbeam interlaced with wisteria and clematis, and divided into squares by vines. The paths are in the form of a cross and represent the axes of the world. The fountain that stands at the centre of the garden is ringed by four quince trees, and its four jets of water symbolise the four rivers of Paradise. Gazebos draped with roses, vines and honeysuckle stand at each end of the paths. It is a place of prayer and meditation, a garden that leads to others:

"an architectural crossroads".

The orchard is where the monks were buried in the Middle Ages. They lie in peace beneath the fruit trees – apple, pear, prune, quince and medlar – the symbols of resurrection.

The area of Petits Fruits (soft fruits) includes a variety of types of espaliers. Redcurrant, blackberry and raspberry bushes are supported by palmettes and cordons. The skilful techniques used to cultivate the fruit are very productive, and utility proves that it can result in beauty.

The Labyrinthe has changed its vocation: originally a kitchen garden, it is now an orchard. Extremely attractive in springtime when all the trees are in flower, it is a place where you can happily get lost – though you will be saved if you can find the centre where the tree of wisdom and life stands. It is an apple tree whose branches have been trained horizontally on a chestnut frame. The Labyrinthe is a marriage of utility and spirituality *par excellence*.

The Jardin de Marie – a pink and white rose garden – pays homage to Mary, mother of Jesus and is an illustration of what is described in the Song of Songs. The roses, lilies and violets have been chosen as they were often used to symbolise the Virgin Mary in illuminated manuscripts.

The Potager Surélevé (Raised vegetable garden) is composed of nine square beds surrounded by woven branches, as seen in

medieval miniatures. This technique brings greater yields as the earth is easily warmed by the sunshine. In autumn the beds offer the pleasurable sight of an abundance of gourds, and aromatic plants are ready to flavour the dishes prepared in the kitchens.

The Jardin des Oliviers is the setting for two old olives, the holy trees most closely linked to the Christian religion. This is a small garden where the visitor can pause in the company of these two silvery ancestors.

The Parterre traces out a geometric shape by means of square beds, which are planted with basic foodstuffs: several varieties of broad beans

and wheat, or leeks and cabbages in winter. The garden is enclosed by the priory walls characterised by lovely regional architecture.

The priory is now being 'reborn' after suffering the vicissitudes of history. Built in the twelfth century by Robert d'Arbrissel (1045–1116), whose name is remembered among Christians for having created the Fontevraud Double Order, the building has suffered fires and pillage. Originally built of wood, it was rebuilt in the sixteenth century and turned into an elegant residence. With its kitchen garden, fishpond, infirmary and chapel, it was a self-sufficient and independent property inhabited

for many years by the order's nuns. The French Revolution brought this to an abrupt end and Orsan was transformed for agricultural use.

When Sonia Lesot and Patrice Taravella arrived, it was in a sad state: dilapidated and overrun by brambles. "Orsan – or at least its buildings – had probably simply been abandoned, and no serious work of reconstruction or restoration had spoiled what remained. Just general negligence had progressively erased its history and characteristics."

It took a lot of faith and energy to imagine it could be returned to the state it is in today,

but it was a gamble that paid off. I am not sure that Patrice Taravella is conscious of it, but his principles are of complete success. For one thing, Orsan is a "useful" garden because visitors are so impressed by its beauty that they want to create their own Orsan. It is true, several people have told me so. Orsan represents the triumph of beauty arising out of utility!

ABOVE *The superbly-trained cloistered pergola with vegetables and vines growing in the enclosed areas.*

LEFT *Roses trained into fans underneath the hornbeam pergola.*

ABOVE *A simple wooden hurdle draws the eye between a hornbeam hedge and pleached limes.*

ABOVE LEFT *Le Prieuré d'Orsan and its imposing turret.*

FAR RIGHT TOP *An olive tree encircled by raised beds made from wooden hurdles.*

OPPOSITE *A grass path between an avenue of lime trees and hornbeam hedge in early spring.*

LEFT Campsis radicans *(or Trumpet vine) trained into a heart shape.*

RIGHT *A rustic wooden bench.*

FAR RIGHT BOTTOM *Pears trained onto a rustic circular framework.*

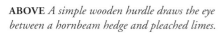

ABOVE *Runner beans, nasturtiums, red cabbage with a wigwam of ipomoea, morning glory and pumpkins drying in the sun.*

RIGHT *Pumpkins laid out to dry and harden the skins so that they can be stored.*

FAR RIGHT TOP *Patrice Taravella.*

FAR RIGHT BOTTOM *A circular rustic seat around an apple tree.*

OPPOSITE RIGHT TOP *A doorway framed by a window of hornbeam.*

OPPOSITE LEFT *A pergola encircles grapevines, a rectangular fountain and rustic arbours covered in quince.*

OPPOSITE RIGHT BOTTOM *A framework holds a bottle in position over a growing pear which is detached when ripe. The bottle is then washed and filled with a pear liqueur.*

LE PRIEURÉ DE ST COSME
Jardins du Prieuré de St Cosme

PHOTOGRAPHY BY DEREK ST ROMAINE AND LIZ EDDISON

Dedicated to the twin saints and healers, Cosmos and Damian, this priory was the residence of Pierre de Ronsard when he was its prior. The rose, which is his flower, grows here in abundance: its elegance, beauty and poetry envelop the ancient stones that have suffered so much. As though they had inherited a healing power from Saint Cosmos himself, the roses seem to dress the wounds of history.

The gardens of the priory-house, the church, cloister and refectory come together like the different verses of a long poem. These contemporary gardens (currently protected,

administered and developed by Vincent Guidault) were created by Jean-Louis Sureau, whose ideas were inspired by the long history of the priory, particularly the Middle Ages: the site itself dates from the twelfth century.

"Thus as you tour the garden you pass from one influence to another: the gardens in the style of *Hortus conclusus*, like the cloister garden, and those in the style of *Hortus delicarum*, like the Jardin des Velours that groups the plants that give the most sensual pleasure," recounts Jean-Louis Sureau.

There are roses in all colours, shapes and sizes. Here you will find every tint that a rose is capable of producing: white, pearly white, purple so dark it is almost black, yellow, orange, crimson. There are botanical roses, ancient and modern roses, climbers, tree roses, rose bushes, ground-covering roses – they are all here.

Right from the entrance the Jardin Rose sets the tone for your visit, with box-lined rose-beds filled with bushes like 'Bonica', and tree roses like 'Iceberg'and 'Crtierion'. The idea behind the Jardin Rose was to create an association between the rose and the Renaissance poet Ronsard. This sixteenth century "Prince of Poets" at

one time actually lived in the priory house next door and extolled the beauty of the grounds.

To the left, the Jardin du Cerceau is named after the engraver Androuet du Cerceau, with the pattern of its gardens based on one of his designs. The perimeter of the garden is lined with tree roses: pink 'Diane de Poitiers', pink 'Joseph Guy' and bright pink 'Sylvie Vartan'. The back enclosure wall, in contrast, is draped with clematis.

Below, the Jardin du Cloitre (The Cloister Garden) is a place for contemplation. It is carpeted with blue lavender that symbolises the ancient gallery. The sky-blue flowers help raise the soul towards the heavens, aided by the columns of a *Cupressus sempervirens* 'Stricta' that rise towards the sky.

Close to the priory ruins, Ronsard's tomb is adorned with 'Pierre de Ronsard' roses. The large trees that give shade to it also provide support for trailing roses like the vigorous 'Rambling Rector' and 'Pauls Himalayan Musk', which envelop them in a white cloud.

The Jardin des Velours is a garden to stimulate the senses. This is where you can feast your eyes on the fruits of the vine, on plum and apricot trees, and swoon to the scent of the roses that cover the pergola – the most spectacular being 'American Pillar', 'New Dawn' and 'Crimson Showers'. Blending in with them are wisterias and laburnums.

The gardens behind the ancient refectory, quite logically, were used for utilitarian

purposes and were laid out next to the kitchens.

The underlying motif of the Verger en Damiers (Chequerboard Orchard) is a series of vertical lines created by roses on supports and staggered rows of fruit trees pruned into cone shapes. All the rose bushes are encircled by squares of box, and each fruit tree (mostly apple) is ringed by a square of grey santolinas.

The kitchen garden is very attractive with its simple, geometric beds. Rectangular at the centre and lozenge-shaped around the perimeter, each bed is lined with small box hedges to separate the different crops. The pear trees are espaliered in the form of 'gobelets', and the apple trees in 'cordons' and 'palmettes'. All is brightly coloured, cheerful and harmonious:

the vegetables, the aromatic, medicinal and seasoning plants, and the fruits, which could have been found here in the sixteenth century.

The Jardin des Senteurs is an assembly of scented plants such as lavender, roses, daphnes and lilies. It is enclosed by large arbours pierced by Romanesque windows to resemble the architecture of the church nearby, which protect the garden from the wind so that the scents given off by the plants are not blown away. On one side it is a curtain of linden trees, whose branches have been elegantly trained on the horizontal, that prevents the town from enjoying this living pot-pourri. The garden has been given a geometric design. Its eight squares, a little higher than the those in the kitchen garden, are lined with box.

Vincent Guidault explains that the Jardin Francis Poulenc was named "for the interest the composer had for this place. He had bought this very small plot beside the church and set Ronsard's poems to music." This small, French garden has box-lined beds, like broderies or a knot garden, inside which are summer flowering annuals, and dominated by 'Lavender Dream' and 'Paul Noël' tree roses.

The Jardin des Fleurs Coupées is rather like a kitchen garden of flowers, with its beds planted with potential bouquets. Peonies, carnations, lilies, roses, sunflowers, and flowers for drying are grown here ready to be cut and brighten the rooms of the priory. The entire wall is espaliered with 'Pierre de Ronsard' roses, which also look very beautiful in a vase.

These gardens, conceived as "prayer mats" for the contemplative life, also offer secular pleasures, with the rose acting as a link between the two.

LEFT *A border of red floribunda roses, 'Sarabande'.*

ABOVE LEFT *'Sweet Juliet' roses as a standard in the potager.*

RIGHT *Borders of pink floribunda roses with white standards edged with low clipped box hedging.*

LEFT *Pink climbing hybrid teas cling to an old ruined archway.*

RIGHT *A view through the pergola with the rambler 'American Pillar' in foreground.*

OPPOSITE TOP *Steps lead down to a sunken garden with banks of roses and cypress trees.*

OPPOSITE BOTTOM LEFT *A border of pink hydrangeas compliment the roses.*

OPPOSITE BOTTOM RIGHT Rosa *'Excelsa'.*

BELOW *Pink and white floribunda roses.*

ABOVE Rosa *'Francois Juranville'*
climbs over the exterior wall.

RIGHT *Red roses on the pergola.*

CENTRE *A double row of*
low box hedges planted with
begonias, standard roses, 'Lavender
Dream', and standard ramblers
in the parterre.

ABOVE *Raindrops on rose 'Manou Meilland'.*

TOP LEFT *A plaque at the entrance to the garden.*

TOP RIGHT *Pale apricot pink roses in a box planter.*

LEFT *Standard roses underplanted with floribundas.*

LE RIVAU
Jardins du château du Rivau

PHOTOGRAPHY BY GARY ROGERS AND DEREK HARRIS

The gardens at Le Rivau, with their many interwoven themes, could not have been restored were it not for the knowledge, courage, and tenacity of Eric Laigneau and his wife Patricia. Their ambitious project began in 1994, and nothing was left to chance. Patricia Laigneau studied at the study Ecole Nationale du Paysage in Versailles, researching the techniques of gardening and architecture, the role and life of plants, the history of the art of gardening, delving into reference books on ancient gardens; she even went on archaeological excavations. In addition to all this, she studied the micro-climates, zones of light and shade, as well as the qualities of the surrounding land – it was important to her to

respect the existing elements of a site, such as local plants and the balance of nature.

The gardens form a single entity with the château, a luminous, imposing and monumental building, whose tufa walls are almost dazzling in the Touraine sunshine. In fact, Patricia Laigneau has cleverly softened this brightness by covering the façade with fan-shaped espaliers of apple trees, appropriately choosing varieties that were popular in the fifteenth and sixteenth centuries. Fig trees and rosebushes at the entrance complete the effect. One rambling rose you will see here is the 'Château du Rivau'. Created by André Eve and named in 2003, it has almost white flowers, followed by fruits in autumn that are much appreciated by the birds.

Owned by the Beauvau family, related to the Counts of Anjou, the château was built between the thirteenth and fifteenth centuries, and both its medieval and Renaissance styles are echoed in the gardens. The Renaissance influence is particularly visible in the lavender knot gardens. These conjure up an almost Mediterranean note of gaiety at the entrance, with the lavenders *Lavandula angustifolia* and *L.* x *intermedia* 'Seal', the santolinas and the cypresses. The intricate designs of knot gardens were very popular in the sixteenth century, and were the forerunners of 'parterres de broderies'. Referring to the Jardin d'En-Bas, Patricia Laigneau explains, "They were inspired by the knot gardens at Blois and Gaillon, which

no longer exist but were illustrated by Jacques Androuet du Cerceau in the sixteenth century in his magnificent collection of engravings, *Les plus excellents bâtiments de France*." As for the Jardin d'En-Haut next to it, she explains, "this is based on the perfect spiral calculated using the Golden Measure, which was very much in vogue in the Renaissance."

While touring the gardens at Le Rivau, you encounter several themes that recur during the walk. At the simplest level, the gardens can be considered as having associations with fairytales, particularly in the case of the Enchanted Forest, where it is easy to imagine sprites nipping through the box, holly, cyclamens and hellebores.

A recurring theme within the Tourangeaux gardens is Renaissance humanist, doctor and writer Rabelais, who is thought to have been born not a stone's throw away at La Devinière, close to Chinon. Rabelais praised Le Rivau in his work *Gargantua*, and reference is made to this in the crescent-shaped kitchen garden 'Potager de Gargantua' in the Cour des Communs. Here raised beds of cucurbitaceous plants are mixed with cabbages, artichokes and thistle-like cardoons. Emphasis is placed on giant varieties, though they are also chosen for their colour and texture. Nasturtiums and dahlias complete the scene. They are called the Tourangeaux gardens because Patricia Laigneau has introduced local Tours varieties of fruits and vines. In this same courtyard she has

constructed frames (which she calls 'crinolines') over which the region's ancient varieties of vine grow.

Another feature seen at Le Rivau – perhaps more often found in modern art gardens – is the placement of sculptures in the undergrowth. One example is the giant work by Basserode called *The Running Forest*, "suggesting a garden that is always changing and that constantly evolves towards its future", as Patricia Laigneau explains.

Two of the themes at Le Rivau are inextricably intertwined: roses and the medieval-style garden, exist here in perfect harmony. The medieval styling was very much dictated by the architecture of the château, with its keep and drawbridge, towers and parapets. Roses, of course, were very popular during the

Middle Ages due to their symbolism of love and beauty, and were frequently illustrated in illuminated manuscripts, whether in the form of a bush, espaliered on trellises, or as simple flower varieties. So their frequent appearances in the gardens at Le Rivau are inkeeping with the period.

And roses are to be seen everywhere: on the walls, climbing, rambling, in bushes and in the flowerbeds. Step off any pathway, and you will find them in front of you; they even have their own gardener to watch over their health and beauty. The delightfully scented rambling varieties 'City of York', 'Albéric Barbier' and 'The Garland' can be seen close up on one of the walls near the Verger de Paradis (Orchard of Paradise).

On the far side of the orchard, in a bed named the Jardin des Philtres d'Amour (Garden of Love Potions), Patricia Laigneau has grouped a cornucopia of scented roses, including 'Old Blush', 'Félicia', 'Félicité Parmentier' and 'Jacques Cartier' among others. The care she has taken over this plantation has resulted in it being nominated a Collection Nationale by the Conservatoire des Collections Végétales Spécialisées. A great success!

The profusion of interlaced strips of osiers, hazel and chestnut trees is also typical of the period. They can be seen at the entrance to the kitchen garden where the raised beds promote the growth of vegetables and utilitarian plants as the earth conserves the warmth of the sun. Woven chestnut strips are placed around citrus fruit pots, whose designs by Patricia Laigneau are inspired by medieval illustrations.

Having a 'damier', a garden with a chequered pattern, was also particularly popular during the Middle Ages. The example at Le Rivau is located near the château. Raised grass-covered squares alternate with square rose-beds. Rather than using ancient varieties or species, this modern interpretation of a damier uses English roses recently developed by David Austin, which have the same charm as ancient

roses in their form and scent but combine the reflowering capabilities of modern roses.

Adjoining Le Damier is the Berceau de Verdure (Green Arbour). Covered with roses and vines, its attractive frame was handmade from chestnut poles and hazel sticks bound together with wicker.

Every medieval garden included an orchard. "The orchard was the pleasure garden in the Middle Ages", explains a specialist of that period, "a place that was always green and shady, planted with fruit and other trees, a sort of copse with some flowers, like a rather disorderly garden, a jumble of roses, honeysuckle and hawthorn mixed with fruit

trees and various shrubs, all of which grew in a sort of wild freedom."

At Le Rivau the orchard, Le Verger de Paradis, is planted with cherry, apple, medlar and almond trees. It is set out in four squares bounded, as was the custom, by paths intersecting in the shape of a cross lined with cherry trees. You can imagine the extravaganza of blossom here in April and the taste of the fruits in autumn: the 'Pépin de Bourgueil', a local variety, is crunchy, scented and sweet, but also sharp – the perfect combination for a cooking apple.

In medieval times, gardens were considered not just on a practical level, but also from a

spiritual and metaphysical aspect. The maze was considered to be representative of all human destiny: a path strewn with errors, setbacks and impasses before one achieves one's goal. Le Rivau's splendid example is best admired from the top of the 'Belvédère.

ABOVE *The lavender garden outside the walled château in summer.*

OPPOSITE LEFT *A detail of the potager with red dahlias, calabasse and marrows.*

OPPOSITE RIGHT *Detail of the Potager de Garguantua in summer.*

OPPOSITE TOP *Panoramic view of the château with the Potager de Garguantua in the foreground.*

OPPOSITE LEFT BOTTOM *A detail of* Brassica kohlrabi *in the potager.*

OPPOSITE RIGHT BOTTOM *The kitchen garden with* Dahlia *'Mascarade' flowers and brassica.*

LEFT *The colourful potager with plated chestnut platforms filled with dahlias, leeks, cabbages and many types of pumkins.*

BELOW *Detail of* Dahlia *'Mascarade'.*

OPPOSITE *The Potager de Garguantua in summer overflowing with flowers and vegetables.*

LEFT *Part of the 'Fairy Garden', the maze 'Alice in Rivauland'.*

BELOW LEFT *Part of the lavender gardens in summer.*

BELOW *A view from the tower over the 'Checkerboard' garden planted with English roses.*

ABOVE *The giant sculptures by the artist Basserode inhabit the 'Running Forest'.*

RIGHT *A corner of the 'Grass Garden' with stipa, Helenium 'Moerheim Beauty', Calamagrostis x acutifloria 'Karl Foerster', Pennisetum 'Moudry' and deschampsia.*

LA SOURCE
Parc floral de La Source

PHOTOGRAPHY BY NICOLA STOCKEN TOMKINS AND DEREK HARRIS

The park at La Source immediately gives a sense of tranquillity. Long, slow steps descend the hill towards a valley. This coomb is protected. The paths wind and the river flows gently. Tall trees, planted carefully to create a balance between deciduous and evergreen species, offer shade and filtered cover to innumerable flowers.

Planted alongside the plateau of Sologne, this park takes its name from the source of the Loiret, which is in actual fact the reappearance of the Loire. It is here that it rises at a particular point: ringed by a circular path at the centre of the park. Because it flows from underground, the temperature of this bubbling water never drops below eight degrees even when the weather is cold, which is why so many flamingos live happily close by.

On walking through the park, the château – overlooking a large lawn adorned with a broderie of box opposite the Miroir – soon becomes apparent. In the eighteenth century, this was home to Lord Bolingbroke, and it was here that he would entertain his circle of men of letters, including Voltaire. The estate changed hands several times over the years until it came into the possession of the City of Orléans and the Conseil Général in 1959.

Five years later a flower park was laid out where the Floralies Internationales exhibition was held in 1967. Today, after years of idleness, its future lies in the hands of the Direction des Espaces Verts de la Ville d'Orléans, which has not only modernised and re-energised the park, but also made it more attractive.

The Parc Floral de La Source is a park for all seasons, not a day passes without a flower coming into blossom. In winter everything is at rest and carefully manicured. The silhouettes of the trees and bushes are clearly outlined as the light and shade interlace between the branches. The undergrowth is carpeted with snowdrops and crocuses and, if you leave the wide paths to observe them more closely, you will discover the camellias around a curve.

Soon these blooms will be replaced by daffodils, narcissi, azaleas and rhododendrons. Then the start of spring will be marked by the arrival of grape hyacinths, hyacinths and, above all, tulips, whether botanical species or hybridised varieties, resembling lilies and peonies, giant, early and late. Planted in huge clumps of the same variety, they are chosen for their bright, shimmering colours. A celebration of spring, this is the time to visit to see them at their most spectacular.

This is also the best time to visit La Rocaille (The Rockery), which lies in front of the iris garden and has just been replanted. Cooled by a stream, the rockery is home to alpine plants, a collection of interesting mosses, and an alpine meadow that is transformed into a carpet of flowers as you approach the Tableau d'Iris.

During the month of May, it is the irises that take pride of place in the Parc Floral de La Source. This collection of irises has been designated a Collection Nationale by the Conservatoire des Collections Nationales Spécialisées. The flowers, from a variety of producers, are rhizomatous or bulbous and have been selected for their colour and novelty. They have been planted fairly freely, as though in a field, as well as in small dishes on tree trunks, which allows them to be seen at eye height. The many varieties (though the majority are *Iris germanica*) make a great show of different shades of blue. Anyone interested in growing irises in their own garden would do well to visit here and note down their favourite varieties. In fact this is true not just for irises; the plants at La Source are carefully and clearly labelled, which enables the visitor to discover and appreciate all sorts of plants, grouped in all manner of combinations.

Roses too occupy a special place at La Source, notably beside the Miroir. Here, they have been grouped by colour: white in the Roseraie de l'Innocence, pink in the Roseraie Romantique, and red in the Roseraie de la Passion. An emphasis has also been placed on scented roses. One rose garden planted with the latest remontant creations is the setting for an annual competition held in September. Climbing roses and rambling roses drape the pergolas, where they are mixed with clematis, which too have been recognised as a Collection Nationale by the CCVS.

The period to visit the Potager is late summer. This is protected by a fine, wave-shaped hedge created by the osier expert Éric Renault, who has mixed various types of willows with yellow, green and brown barks. The kitchen garden contains all sorts of standard vegetables, as well as Chinese artichokes, parsnips and Jerusalem artichokes, which are cultivated in rotation. There are also aromatic and flowering plants typical of kitchen gardens, such as marigolds and nasturtiums, which, like everything here, are grown organically. Close by is a trapezoidal orchard containing raspberry, redcurrant and strawberry bushes and traditional fruit trees: figs, apricots, quince, plums and medlars.

The stars of the summer and autumn are unquestionably the dahlias growing close by. Planted in a garden in the shape of an arc, they are present in all colours, sizes and forms: single-, anemone- and peony-flowered, pompom, cactus, collarette and decorative dahlias. The Parc de la Source is an excellent place to study these flowers and to choose one's personal favourites.

Every gardener wishing to increase his or her knowledge of the fundaments of gardening and the large plant families, which are always being expanded with new varieties, should make a point of visiting the Parc Floral de La Source.

RIGHT *Woodland in spring filled with swathes of tulips and narcissi.*

ABOVE *In spring a bank of trees engulfed in fragrant white narcissi.*

RIGHT *White and red hyacinths with a* Magnolia x soulangeana *in the background.*

MIDDLE *The 'Dahlia Garden' flowering in early autumn.*

FAR TOP RIGHT *A small summerhouse, its roof clad in moss, edges with photinia and mahonia.*

FAR BOTTOM RIGHT *In the 'Source Garden' a pool and rockery with ferns, skimmia, ageratum, tagetes, begonia and salvia.*

ABOVE *Filled with surprises, this wide path wanders past beautiful herbaceous borders and trees.*

FAR LEFT *The sculpture* La Source *by Volti, lit by the evening sun.*

LEFT *Banana plant,* Musa *in a large container.*

RIGHT *The château sits above a tracery of box hedges overlooking the lake and fountain.*

ABOVE *In a corner of the potager is a willow summerhouse with a decorated wooden door.*

FAR LEFT *La Roseraie du Miroir: a contemporary rose garden with beds of perennials and roses trained along pergolas.*

OPPOSITE TOP RIGHT *Le Potager Extraordinaire, a kitchen garden of fruit, vegetables and herbs guarded by a scarecrow.*

OPPOSITE BOTTOM RIGHT *A clearing with summer borders with swathes of echinacea, daylilies, stipa and Shasta daisies.*

LEFT *Terracotta pots filled with fuchsias towards a line of plane trees.*

TALCY
Verger de collection du château de Talcy

PHOTOGRAPHY BY NICOLA STOCKEN TOMKINS

For miles and miles the road wends its way endlessly through village after village and muted, dull-coloured wheat fields. Then, finally, you arrive in Talcy, with its fine château and roofs of silvery slate… what a wonderful contrast!

This is a feudal residence to enchant the eyes, its air of mystery enticing you to enter, explore and uncover its secrets.

From inside there are views both to the north and to the south. From its reception rooms, and above all from its raspberry-coloured salon, your gaze takes in on one side a simple allée lined with linden trees *(Tilia cordata)*, and on the other side remarkably well-constructed and ordered gardens with a path of small raspberry bushes right at their centre.

The history of Talcy has included golden ages of long gowns, poets and muses, and a life of

self-sufficiency and independence.

Bernard Salviati, who had links with the Medici family, acquired the house in 1517, and it became the country residence for his daughter Cassandre. Having met and fallen in love with Cassandre (though he did not visit Talcy), the poet Pierre de Ronsard recounted his passion for her in his poems *Amours de Cassandre*, which remain famous to this day.

Cassandre's niece, Diane Salviati, who also made her home at Talcy, won the love of Agrippa d'Aubigné. Unfortunately, he was Protestant and she was Catholic, making marriage an impossibility during this time of the Wars of Religion. And so all that was left to Agrippa d'Aubigné, was to declare his passion for Diane in verse.

We know from a seventeenth century plan of the estate that the gardens enjoyed by the Salviati women were similar to their current form, with their square symmetrical beds arranged the length of the main axis.

The property remained in the Salviati family until the end of the seventeenth century when it was made an elegant and productive country residence by the Burgeat family. Within the bounds of the park they found an orchard planted with apple, pear, almond, peach and apricot trees, a vegetable garden, a vineyard, a well, a dovecote, a fishpond, several barns, some kennels, a press, and everything needed to live in self-sufficiency. They undertook works to embellish the building and its gardens,

replanted the orchard and employed several gardeners. It was a period of abundance, beauty and prosperity.

The estate remained intact until the nineteenth century when it was broken up. In its new limited form it passed into the hands of the Stapfer family, but they sold it to the French State in 1932. In the 1990s it was decided to restore the gardens, a project that was responsible, among other developments, for the disappearance of the staggered rows of linden trees on the first terrace, and for the plantation of a collection of fruit trees.

The gardens lie on two levels. They are open, well constructed, well designed, well balanced and in complete harmony with the château. Laid out by a knowledgeable eye, their refined organisation is complemented by the poetry of the place: the right proportions; the exposure; the light; its history; perhaps the rhymes and pretty thoughts of famous poets still hang in the air.

For a good understanding of the gardens, you will need to follow the main axis, which begins in the ancient Allée d'Honneur, passes through the château and terraces, and opens a long perspective as far as the wood that overlooks the Petite Beauce, passing by several very beautiful European black pines.

Below the keep and its turrets sits the Cour d'Honneur, the main courtyard, featuring an elegant gallery inspired by the one in the château in Blois and a well draped with 'Pierre

de Ronsard' roses. Flowerbeds, planted with bulbs and pansies in spring, and sage, ageratum, nigella and verbena in summer. On the other side of the wall is the "Basse-cour" or farmyard, which is enclosed by the gardener's cottage, the kennels, pigeon house, press, and barn.

From here a very fine gate leads to five steps, at the bottom of which you will find yourself on the main axis of the gardens. Two large symmetrical beds lie on either side of the main axis on the first terrace. These are ornamental gardens recently restored under the direction of Patrick Ponsot, Chief Architect of the Monuments Historiques, and Joelle Weill, a landscape artist, who together brought them into line with modern taste. They have successfully updated the design of the 'broderies', or 'knot gardens' while reinterpreting them. The perimeter is defined by low hedges of box; inside, arabesques of filled and empty areas are formed by different shrubs: dogwood, privet and viburnums have been cut flat to a height lower than the box and mixed together to create swirling patterns. Some of them flower while others bear fruit. It is a lovely idea. A few grasses emerge amid the interlaced plants, including miscanthus.

Each year Claude Bichon creates a composition on either side of the pathway of pretty annual flowering plants, such as centauries, calliopsis, cosmos, sunflowers and achilleas, which present their rich colours all through the summer.

The second level is reached down a lovely crescent flight of nine steps, leading to the kitchen gardens set out in squares on either side. The central pathway is planted with cherry trees and soft fruit, and lined with nepeta. The raspberries are well represented with such fine varieties as 'Violette', 'Bois Blanc', 'Sucrée de Metz' and 'Rouge de Sauron', and there are also redcurrants, blackcurrants, and gooseberries.

The kitchen garden is ordered in large squares lined with box hedges arranged symmetrically around the main axis. Some of the squares are planted with mixtures of annuals, others mostly with phacelias, and some with edible plants or lavender – either 'Dutch' *L.* x *intermedia* or 'Dwarf Blue' *L. angustifolia.*

On the left, the gardens evaporate into the farm land planted with rows of fruit trees. On the right, the unwalled orchard is planted symmetrically with apple, pear, peach and nectarine trees.

At the centre of the kitchen garden stands a group of carefully trained fruit trees: in espaliers in the form of palmettes obliques, croisillons (Belgian fence), cordons simples (single horizontals), tridents (three-branch candelabra), cordons doubles superposés (double horizontals), and four- or five-branch palmettes verriers.

Three mown pathways radiate from a centre point ending in a ha-ha, enabling the gaze to range unimpeded towards the Petite Beauce. The wood is planted with snowdrops and wild plants, offering refuge to game.

In spring the charm of Talcy is heightened by the fruit blossom, and in autumn it is coloured by the fruits, changes that only add to this place's poetry.

LEFT *View of the potager demonstrating the different ways in which fruit trees can be trained.*

RIGHT *Château de Talcy rises above its restored kitchen garden where fruit trees are espaliered in different traditional styles.*

ABOVE *A gnarled old cherry tree is laden in blossom in spring, beneath its boughs the espaliered fruit trees are still dormant after winter.*

LEFT *Cowslips* (Primula veris) *are naturalised throughout the meadows and fields at Talcy.*

MIDDLE *Dating from the thirteenth century, the Château de Talcy looks out over its potager filled with spring blossom from apple, pear and cherry.*

OPPOSITE TOP *A box-edged square is filled with undulating, tightly clipped domes of lavender, in sharp contrast to the flat landscape beyond.*

OPPOSITE BOTTOM *Cherry blossom takes centre stage in spring, the Château de Talcy fading into the background.*

TOP *A heritage variety pear* (Poire Premier Curee) *is trained in a trident shape.*

ABOVE *A heritage variety apple* (Pommier Reinette Des Capucins) *is trained in an espalier, in a four-branched Palmette Vernier manner.*

RIGHT *The apple Jonagold is trained in a criss-crossed Croisillons style.*

ABOVE *Claude Bichon, curator at Château de Talcy, inspects the autumn's crop of heritage fruit.*

RIGHT *An old apple variety (Pommier Reinette Des Capucins) is trained in an espalier of four branches in the Palmette Verrier style, held in place by wires and wooden lathes.*

TOP RIGHT *By early autumn, a central path is largely engulfed by cosmos, at its end a glimpse of the flat fields of brown earth beyond.*

FAR RIGHT *Enclosed in lines of clipped box hedges, interwoven domes of lavender lie in front of the ancient château.*

TOURS
Parcs et jardins de la ville de Tours

PHOTOGRAPHY BY LIZ EDDISON AND DEREK ST ROMAINE

LES PREBENDES D'OE

Here, in this pocket of air and chlorophyll in the city, with its charming, old-French atmosphere, several epochs meet and jostle up against one another.

This creation, in a shape that approximates a diamond, was designed as a tranquil and romantic place by the Bühler brothers – Eugène (1822–1907) and Denis (1811–1890) – with ponds and tall trees, and statues of the local poets Racan and Ronsard. The gardens now also boast a contemporary tribute to Senegalese poet, politician and intellectual Léopold Senghor. This surprising and very clever sculpture by Michel Audiard immortalises the

great man, who studied in Tours and often came to sit on the benches in this park.

The Bühler brothers, who designed the gardens between 1872 and 1874, created a number of parks in an irregular style, in particular the Parc de La Tête d'Or in Lyons. Les Prebendes d'Oé in Tours was laid out on what had originally been swamps, before becoming market gardens. The land had a small stream running through it, which was eventually formed into a canal. At one time the land belonged to the Provost d'Oé, who drew his stipend, or prebend, from the small village of Notre-Dame d'Oé, where he lived, close to Tours.

The Bühlers planted groups of large trees of the same species: planes, limes, cedars and sequoias tower over a shrubby undergrowth of aucubas, mahonias and hydrangeas and contrast with the horizontal stretches of lawns and ponds. Some specimens are planted in isolation to emphasise their rarity: a Turkish hazel (*Corylus colurna*), a persimmon from Italy (*Diospyros lotus*), and a yellow wood (*Cladrastris lutea*), each bearing a label as though they were personalities.

The ponds are straddled by Rocaille-style bridges that are reminiscent of the ornamentation at Buttes Chaumont. Many of the rustic garden decorations are made in cement, but formed so as to imitate wood with its veins and knots. A small island is planted with bald cypresses and their pneumataphores.

The Petit Kiosque and the Kiosque à Musique, where concerts were once given, resonate with the echoes of times past

THE BOTANIC GARDEN

The Botanic Garden in Tours is an ideal place to learn about plants, whether you are a student or plant-lover.

Created in 1863 by a chemist, Jean-Anthyme Margueron, with the assistance of the Hôpital de Tours and the Ecole Préparatoire de Pharmacie, this garden is a valuable tool for students of pharmacy.

The first part of the garden, at the entrance and close to the glasshouses, spreads on either side of a main pathway that features a pool at its centre. This section of the garden is very organised and compartmentalised.

On the left is the Jardin de l'Evolution, which describes the evolution of the large families of plants in the form of a table or chart. It also teaches pharmaceutical students the organisation of botanical classification. It encompasses a collection of hardy perennials classed by family, a square bed of bulb plants, and a wall against which espaliered rose-bushes, jasmines, honeysuckles and passion flowers are lined. There is also a *Fremontodendron*, originally from California, which produces beautiful large yellow flowers.

On the right, the Jardin des Plantes de Collection presents ornamental plants in the settings in which they feel most at home: there

are heathland plants like rhododendrons, azaleas, maples, camellias and hydrangeas, and a fine collection of heathers; a fern field in the half-shade displays arborescent ferns; perennials happy in peat bog terrain or cool earth include Siberian irises and hostas; Mediterranean plants include rockroses and eucalyptuses; and an alpine garden with dwarf conifers takes the form of a rockery with a waterfall that feeds a winding stream.

The pool contains a lovely collection of pink or blue flowered water-lilies, and lotuses whose beauty is at its greatest in July and August. This is a place that invites contemplation.

The second part of the garden is an

irregularly shaped park with a stream running through it and a pond that encircles the garden of medicinal plants. The park, with more than 150 genera and species of trees from all five continents, is in fact more like an arboretum. Among the most remarkable are a *Gingko biloba* whose trunk measures 7 metres round at ground level, an impressive tulip tree, a cork oak, and an *Araucaria imbricata* originally from California.

The Jardin des Plantes Médicinales is very lovely. Its charm, like all gardens of this type, lies in the fact that its plants are for the most part aromatic. Furthermore, their foliage is often persistent and in the grey and green ranges of tones, which imparts a feeling of gentleness to the garden as a whole. In geometric beds more or less regularly shaped and enclosed by hornbeam hedges, the plants are grouped by therapeutic properties: antitumoral, antiseptic, sedative, or tinctorial.

As you return to the glasshouses via the meandering paths through the trees, you will discover all kinds of animals: fallow deer, dwarf goats, peacocks, tortoises. The glasshouses are currently being restored. One is dedicated to producing plants for special occasions, and another to protecting spectacular exotic plants.

Although is worth setting aside several hours to really explore the botanic garden, the beauty of the place also allows you simply to wander through it to admire the plants, flowers and the glorious colours.

ABOVE *Spring bedding display comprising dark crimson early tulips with crimson bellis, dark red primulas, white forget-me-nots and white violas.*

OPPOSITE LEFT *Blue and white bedding display including ageratum, begonias and tagetes.*

OPPOSITE RIGHT *Curved borders of spring bedding including narcissus, polyanthus and pansies.*

ABOVE *White lily flowered tulips in combination with pink bellis, yellow violas and the silver leaves of* Cineraria maritima *in a border by the edge of the lake.*

TOP RIGHT *A mixture of different coloured primulas with crimson bellis, white and yellow trumpet tulips dwarfed by an enormous giant redwood tree and a 'rustic' arbour made of concrete.*

BOTTOM RIGHT *A weeping willow at one end of the lake and a pathway edged by a 'rustic' log fence made from concrete.*

OPPOSITE LEFT *Ducks beside a small pond shaded by a Californian redwood.*

OPPOSITE TOP RIGHT *Silver birch trees planted in a group close together show off their bark to great effect in spring.*

OPPOSITE BOTTOM RIGHT *Purple rhododendron and new leaves of an* Acer japonicum.

ABOVE *Pelargoniums beside a sheet steel fretwork portrait of the Senegalese poet, politician and intellectual Léopold Senghor.*

LEFT *A gardener watering a display of regal pelargoniums and a standard bougainvillea in the shade of a red oak* (Quercus rubra).

TOP RIGHT *Early morning ducks on the lake.*

RIGHT *Early morning sunlight trying to penetrate the massive canopy of giant redwoods.*

VALMER
Jardins du château de Valmer

PHOTOGRAPHY BY GARY ROGERS AND NICOLA STOCKEN TOMKINS

In winter, when Valmer is divested of its flowers and swathed in mist, it is only just possible to make out the silhouette of the architecture of its gardens. The profile forms the suggestion of a piano, with the keys descending the terraced slope of the hills, down towards the beds of its kitchen garden and the river valley. The manner in which this garden adapts to the great drop in height is similar to that of the Cent Marches at Versailles as it descends the slope to the Pièce d'Eau des Suisses, or, on a smaller scale, like the grassy steps opposite the Château de Dampierre in Yvelines.

Ash-grey, white, ochre beige, iced chestnut – all the tonalities are soft, and the colours of

the stones harmonise with those of the boughs. Winter is a beautiful season at Valmer.

With its sixteenth-century terraces, its vases, urns and fountains, the monumental gates and finely carved gateways in the balustrades, and the sense of gaiety, it is as though one has been transported back to a villa of the Italian Renaissance.

The main château, constructed in the seventeenth century, was destroyed in a fire. Alix de Saint-Venant has rebuilt it in yew on the same site. As for the Petit Valmer that stands just behind, it is a replica of the château and is alive and well.

Nothing is known of the original designer of the gardens. They are laid out around two axes. The first, running north-south, begins in a majestic crescent-shaped avenue of chestnuts planted in two rows. It crosses the first courtyard, runs alongside the outbuildings, passes across the ditches and Florentine Terraces, and continues towards the park where Alix de Saint-Venant has planted collections of rare trees, including a collection of oaks, which will one day form a veritable arboretum.

The second axis, which runs east-west, originates on the High Terrace where a series of tree-covered walks forms a maze, crosses the Florentine Terraces, then the Terrasse du Vase de Lorraine, descends a flight of steps, spans the Terrasse de Leda, arrives on the Terrasses des Vases d'Anduze, and meets the kitchen garden.

Alix de Saint-Venant started the restoration

of the kitchen garden in 2000, and thanks to her research it has developed into a conservatory of ancient species.

"I started from two books published by Vilmorin," she recounts, "*Les Plantes Potagères* and *Les Fleurs de Pleine Terre*, which were their seed catalogues, publication of which began at the end of the nineteenth century. I wanted to search out the varieties grown in the past – with three objectives in mind: to bring together edible plants that are also lovely to look at; to conserve the botanical heritage by protecting their seeds; and to share the collections with visitors, thereby encouraging them to cultivate them, not just for pleasure but also so that they might diffuse them in turn, and thus preserve them."

The kitchen garden is divided into four squares around a pool at the centre. The squares are named after famous people from the gardening world of the past: Vilmorin, who was the creator of the arboretums at Verrières and Les Barres, and the famous seed merchant in the Quai de La Mégisserie in Paris; Parmentier, who discovered the nutritive value of the potato in the eighteenth century, and developed its cultivation during the reign of Louis XVI; La Quintinye, who created the Potager du Roy at Versailles; and Pailleux and Bois, who worked on vegetables and introduced, amongst others, the Japanese artichoke (*Stachys affinis*) into France in 1882. Each of these squares is sub-divided into smaller squares in which vegetables,

aromatic plants, and edible plants such as borage and hemerocallis are planted in rows.

And there are many curiosities to be found in this garden: local varieties like the Sucrin de Tours, which is a delicious round melon with orangey-red flesh; then there are fifty or so types of mint; green manures made from clover and lacy phacelia; pink, violet, white and yellow radishes; the Yacon strawberry (*Polymnia edulis*), whose edible roots are like those of the dahlia; and Oca (*Oxalis tuberosum*), whose roots are also edible.

Something is always happening at Valmer. In winter, the frost or snow sugar-coat the topiaries. In spring, the terraces are a mass of bulb flowers and pansies, and the kitchen garden is on the rise. This is the time of salads

and peas. The squares are coloured blue and
green, and are ringed with nepeta, and soon
the wisteria will bloom on the chapel wall. In
summer, the greatest spectacle is in the kitchen
garden among the tomatoes and aubergines,
but also in the ditches where Alix de Saint-
Venant has planted very beautiful hydrangeas,
including *Hydrangea sargentiana* and *Hydrangea
quercifolia* 'Snow Queen'. In August the Pergola
des Gourdes is a dramatic sight, draped in
gourds of every colour and shape. In autumn,
the vines command attention, thousands
of Neapolitan cyclamens unroll their pink
carpet, and the flame-coloured foliage of the
liquidambars and bald cypresses dazzle the eye;
the kitchen garden has achieved maturity, the
root vegetables are ready, and the pears and
apples are ripe on the bough.

The 'gardening' continues in the vineyards,
where Aymar de Saint-Venant exercises his
talent as a wine grower. He returned the vines
to cultivation some years ago, and today is
rewarded with their fruit, which makes a
delicious Vouvray wine.

Valmer is a garden set amongst vineyards.
The practically straight lines of the vines find
their echo in the straightness of the terraces,
recalling the tradition in which Italian gardens
are first shaped and fabricated before being
planted. This phrase by Marella Agnelli on the
gardens of Italian villas might well apply to
those at Valmer: "Behind every garden there is
a long, long history in which the poetical ideals
of several generations are interlaced".

LEFT *Autumn swathes of* Cyclamen
hederifolium *in pink and white.*

ABOVE LEFT *A view across the Italian
Terrace to the château.*

RIGHT *Looking down from the Italian
terrace onto La Terrasse des Fontaines
Florentines and up to Le Petit Valmer.*

ABOVE *Giant yew with cosmos, cleome and a statue of Cupid.*

LEFT *A bank of lavender, box, yew and roses.*

RIGHT *Yew framed view of La Terrasse des Fontaines Florentines.*

MIDDLE *A view over the 'Prairie Flowering Fields' towards the 'Tour de l'Ane' with cosmos and lavatera.*

OPPOSITE TOP *In the potager, a path of Nepeta 'Six Hills Giant' leads to the main garden.*

OPPOSITE BOTTOM *Border detail of cosmos 'Sonata ou Versailles' and* cleome spinosa.

TOP *Historic kitchen garden with apples trained in a single cordon above catmint.*

ABOVE *A section of the 110m long pergola which contains the Lagernaria National Collection of Gourds.*

RIGHT *The Florentine fountain which is the centerpiece of the lower terrace, with a border of 'Noir de Toscane' and 'Green peacock' ornamental cabbages.*

ABOVE *A view of the castle from the middle terrace over the beds of ornamental cabbage and Zinnia 'Tapis Persan'.*

LEFT *A shelter in the potager for insects such as bees.*

VILLANDRY
Jardins du château de Villandry

PHOTOGRAPHY BY LIZ EDDISON, DEREK ST ROMAINE AND DEREK HARRIS

 However many visits you pay to Villandry, your sense of wonder never diminishes in the face of such balance, harmony and perfection. Even if you think you know the place, you are mistaken as it changes with the light, the seasons and the hour of the day.

Villandry can be seen over and over, and it will be different every time. It is a kitchen garden associated with ornamental gardens. But it is also a garden of colours carefully blended so that they sing in the Touraine sunshine. In the Loire Valley colours respond differently, especially in the presence of a white stone château.

So how should this garden be viewed? Is it an exercise in geometry, with its square beds

forming the shape of the cross and its designs of Moorish box that fit into one another?

Or is it an historic garden? Its history abounds with the great and famous, and with restorations. Could it be a study on trimmed forms, with its disk-tiered topiaries, small, straight-as-a-die box hedges, and its rows of perfectly groomed lime trees?

What if the gardens are simply an extension of Henri Carvallo's collection of paintings? (The four canvases representing the Marquis de Castellane, a former owner of Villandry, visiting the Ottoman Empire in the seventeenth century, are on show in the château.)

Or, what if the gardens are just a horizontal work of art? One that you can admire from the windows in the reception rooms, just like the paintings that adorn the walls of the château's many salons, or like a tapestry or a carpet?

Whatever they are, the gardens have their roots in the Middle Ages and the Renaissance. They were created by Joachim Carvallo who took his inspiration from the plans drawn by Androuet du Cerceau in his book *Les plus excellents bâtiments de France*.

But now they are also the gardens of the present and future as Henri Carvallo has just created new gardens inspired by an engraving made by his great-grandfather. Carvallo's original idea has been adapted to the taste of the day by Alix de Saint-Venant, the botanist, landscape gardener and owner of the château of Valmer, along with Louis Benech, one of

the greatest French landscape architects, whose richly poetic vision is illustrated in the interplay of plants.

To explain the historic evolution of the gardens, Henri Carvallo lays out several plans on the table. The first shows Villandry in the seventeenth century, when its ornamental gardens were already in their current place, but the kitchen garden was just half the size of today's because the village occupied more space. This was the Villandry of the first owner, Jean Le Breton.

A second plan, also from the seventeenth century, shows the Villandry of Monsieur de Castellane, who bought up a part of the village. He demolished the houses on the west side and extended the gardens until the church found itself on the boundary between the village and the garden.

A third plan shows the estate around 1840, with the château surrounded by a landscaped garden. This was still the case when Joachim Carvallo bought the estate in 1906. He undertook some excavation work during which the foundations of the retaining wall of the ancient terraces were found. And this discovery enabled him to rebuild the ancient gardens on the basis of the gardens of the Renaissance. This phase of development continued until 1918.

The tour of the current estate begins with a visit to the château itself so that you can study the gardens. In particular a corner where the ornamental gardens and kitchen garden can

both be seen. They are both a work of art in their own right and astonishingly beautiful. Everything is just right: the layout, the colours, the cut forms, the proportions, the perfectionist work of the gardeners, the relationships of the perspectives, and the excellent health of the plants...everything is consistent.

The gardens are built on different levels. The kitchen garden is the lowest. It is divided into nine squares decorated with clearly defined geometric patterns – variations on the theme of the cross. The paths are covered with a local gravel known as "mignonnette" and cross at right angles in each square at a basin framed by four trellised bowers that support climbing roses. The perimeter of the garden is decorated with trellis-work and cordons of apple trees. The squares are planted with the season's vegetables chosen on the basis of their colours. In spring there are green-blue-grey Primero cabbages, green lettuce, green or purple Salad Bowl oakleaf, red oakleaf and broad beans; these are accompanied by forget-me-nots, pansies and wallflowers.

The Jardins d'Ornement and Jardin des Simples lie on the first level terrace, the first are close to the château, the second to the church.

The first section of the ornamental gardens is the Jardin d'Amour, with its box hedges and elegant topiary forms enclosing tulips and forget-me-nots in spring, and begonias in summer. Its four squares symbolise four forms of love: l'Amour Tragique, with its two-edged swords and daggers; l'Amour Adultère, with the theme of the fan expressing a fickle spirit; l'Amour Tendre, with masks that conceal the swapping of sweet nothings; and l'Amour Passionné, with its broken hearts.

The following bed represents the crosses of monastic gardens: the Maltese cross, the cross of Languedoc and the cross of the Basque country.

The second section is devoted to music, with three squares that describe stylised instruments. The colour harmonies here are gentler, and the box encloses lavenders and grey santolinas.

The long Jardin des Simples (medicinal plants) marries the utility of the kitchen garden with the decoration of the ornamental gardens, with its yew hedges all cut in tiers of disks. A long allée is decorated with three circles that diminish in size. The quarters of each circle are planted with aromatic herbs: absinthe, fennel, oregano, tarragon and thyme diffuse their scents in the air.

Henri Carvallo's new gardens are located between the hornbeam maze and the Jardin d'Eau, with a pool in the form of a Louis XV mirror from where water flows down a series of steps to the moat. The old green meadow has been divided into three parts: one is planted with apple trees and is for children to play in, another is dedicated to the sun, and the third to clouds.

The Jardin du Soleil was inspired by a sketch made by Joachim Carvallo in 1924 for a project he never followed up. Henri Carvallo asked Arnaud de Saint-Jouan, chief architect of the Monuments Historiques, to design a fountain for the garden, and Alix de Saint-Venant designed an eight-pointed star. Louis Benech selected a multitude of warm-hued perennials "that evoke a sky at sunset or sunrise", including crocuses, achilleas, spiraeas, gaillardias, coreopsis, and astrantias. "These warm, straw colours are complemented by leaves that are either prawn-coloured ('Prinz Handjéry' and 'Brillantissimum' maples) or

fiery ('Gold Flame' *Spiraea japonica*) and by a rose that changes colour during the hours that it is open: first red, then peach, turning to hot pink". This is the 'Mutabilis' variety of *Rosa chinensis*.

The Jardin des Nuages, created by Louis Benech, forms the antechamber to the Jardin du Soleil and is the only garden at Villandry not based on straight lines. "Its paths glide like currents of air between the large grey, white, pale blue and violet triangles, announcing either the dawn or twilight," says Benech,

explaining his use of blue delphiniums and nepetas, carnations, silvery lychnis, lavenders, rockroses, rue and penstemons.

These gardens lie on the highest terrace, brushing the sky and stars, reflecting Joachim Carvallo's ambition of giving his gardens a spiritual dimension in affirmation that art and beauty elevate the soul.

Villandry can also be thought of as being inspired by monastic gardens, this style being symbolised by the tree roses in the kitchen garden that represent a monk digging his

vegetable bed – the monk, in close rapport with the world above, is applying its rules here below.

Perhaps that is how the gardens at Villandry should be viewed: as a reflection of heaven.

LEFT *A meadow of cosmos.*

ABOVE *View across the 'Jardin d'Amour showing the Languedoc and the Maltese cross filled with red begonias.*

FAR LEFT TOP *Perovskia planted in the 'Music Garden'.*

FAR LEFT BOTTOM *Early spring tulips and clipped topiary in the Jardin des Simples.*

LEFT *A vine grows over the pergola which runs alongside the canal.*

BELOW *The Jardin des Simples in spring viewed though an avenue of lime trees.*

RIGHT *In early spring the new lush green growth shows in the Jardin d'Amour which is planted with early tulips.*

BOTTOM RIGHT *Taxus topiary and buxus hedging in the 'Music Garden' with a view to a fountain.*

FAR RIGHT *The château viewed through the new growth on a pollarded branch of a lime tree.*

PREVIOUS PAGE *Panoramic view of the kitchen gardens in spring.*

BELOW *View of the Jardin d'Amour planted with begonias.*

RIGHT *The square representing l'Amour Adultère with the château behind.*

OPPOSITE TOP LEFT *View over the formal Jardin d'Amour with summer bedding of begonias.*

OPPOSITE BOTTOM LEFT *The square representing l'Amour Adultère planted with begonias.*

FAR RIGHT TOP *Symmetry in the borders of the potager.*

FAR RIGHT BOTTOM *A central fountain in the Jardin d'Amour.*

ABOVE *Sprinklers in the evening light watering the grass in the Jardin d'Eau.*

LEFT *Ornamental cabbages in the late summer potager.*

RIGHT *Standard roses, cabbages, ornamental cabbages and begonias make a colourful late summer potager.*

FAR RIGHT TOP *Formal borders with low clipped buxus hedging enclose ornamental cabbages.*

FAR RIGHT BOTTOM *Cabbages, standard roses and tomatoes make a colourful display in the potager.*

MARIE-FRANCOISE VALERY

The author, is one of France's most distinguished garden writers. She is the author of *French Garden Style, Splendeur des Jardins de Normandie, Jardens de France en fleurs* and *Jardins du Moyen Age* as well as contributing features for the major gardening press.

LIZ EDDISON

After leaving Harrow School of Art, Liz went on to work in the photographic department of Sotheby Auctioneers and then for advertising photographer Bob Wallis as an assistant and stylist. For some years following this she became a photographers' agent.

Frustrated with being on the business side of the industry and not behind the lens, she later decided to combine her passion for gardening with photography, alongside freelance picture research. Her photographs are published internationally in books and magazines and she is a co-founder of The Garden Collection.

Liz now lives in Harrow with her partner Roger, and her son Sam is the creative director of The Garden Collection.

DEREK HARRIS

Derek Harris is an internationally-recognised, and award-winning flower, garden and landscape photographer. His work appears in books, magazines, calendars, stationery, and limited and open edition prints. His photography is creative and based on the principles he learnt during his art and design training. Initially attracted by the spontaneity of photography and the beauty, colours and magic of nature, he now tries to capture it all with his camera so it can be shared with others.

Derek has received many awards for both his photography and design, notably winning the Photographic Greeting Card of the Year prize for two years running. He has won the Garden Photograph of the Year competition (awarded by the Garden Writers' Guild) and was chosen by the Garden Photographers' Association for the Photographers' Choice Picture of the Year.

As well as this, Derek's work has been exclusively used in a number of books including the best-selling *Monet at Giverny*, the acclaimed *Westonbirt – Celebration of the Seasons* and the award winning *Cornwall's Great Gardens*.

His series of high-quality studio flower portraits have been awarded four Royal Horticultural Society gold medals. His limited edition prints are now in private collections in the UK, Europe, USA, Canada and Australia.

GARY ROGERS

Gary Rogers was German Photographer of the Year 2007.

He travels extensively through Europe and America photographing every garden he visits with an enthusiasm and energy envied by many.

Before embracing garden photography full time, Gary won awards for his work in many different areas: fashion, architecture, TV news stills and theatre; he also covered the lifestyle stories of well known stars and pop groups.

In 1999 he won the Features Photographer of the Year award from the Garden Writers' Guild for the book *The Garden of Chatsworth*.

Based in, Germany, he is a major contributor to the magazines *Schöner Wohnen, S/W Decoration, Häuser*, and *Living at Home*. He also supplies images to the major garden book publishers in the UK, USA and Germany. Two recently published titles including his work are *Design in the Garden*, by Ursula Barth and *Garden Magic*, by Gisela Keil.

Gary was born in New Zealand and is married, living in Hamburg, Germany with his wife Karin, a well known picture editor. They have two daughters, Jaana and Nadja, who are no strangers to their father's cameras and packed bags.

DEREK ST ROMAINE

Derek St Romaine is one of the UK's leading horticultural and gardening photographers. He trained as a graphic designer at Harrow School of Art and spent many years working as an art director in publishing. He switched over to photography in 1985 and specialized in food photography at his Chelsea studio before turning his attention to plant and garden photography.

He is married and lives and works in Surrey. He and his wife Dawn are passionate gardeners and their garden has appeared in many books and magazines worldwide. The garden is open for charity under the National Garden Scheme and is also listed in *The Good Gardens Guide*.

Derek's work is always in demand, and he supplies all the major gardening magazines and book publishers in the UK, as well as many in Europe and America.

In 1993 and 1996 he won Garden Writers' Guild awards for plant portrait and garden photography. In 1998 he was awarded a gold medal by the Royal Horticultural Society for an exhibition of Garden and Plant Photography. In 2001 and 2003 he was voted Garden Photographer of the Year at the Garden Writers' Guild awards, scooping the top prize for photography. In 2005 he was awarded joint runner-up in the annual GPA exhibition 'Features' category. In 2006 he was runner-up in the Royal Botanic Gardens 'Kew' category.

NICOLA STOCKEN TOMKINS

Nicola both photographs and writes about lovely gardens, renowned gardeners and nurseries throughout the British Isles, specialising in features for magazines and newspapers throughout the world. Her images, depicting every aspect of garden life, also appear in books and on calendars and greetings cards.

Nicola is married with one son, and in her spare time she windsurfs, plays the piano and watches life go by on the River Thames where she lives with her husband, two cats and any number of passing, itinerant ducks.

THE GARDEN COLLECTION

The five photographers from this book all have their work represented by The Garden Collection, a photographic agency, which was started to give an online presence for some of the world's leading garden photographers. The Garden Collection is committed to promoting its individual photographers' unique collections as a rights managed source of images. Photographs from this book and other work by the photographers can be licensed from The Garden Collection website at: www.garden-collection.com